THE MORNINGSTAR APPROACH TO INVESTING

THE MORNINGSTAR APPROACH TO INVESTING

WIRING INTO THE MUTUAL FUND REVOLUTION

ANDREW LECKEY

Foreword by Louis Rukeyser

WARNER BOOKS

A Time Warner Company

Warner Books, Inc., 1271 Avenue of the Americas, New York, NY 10020

W A Time Warner Company

Printed in the United States of America
First Printing: January 1997
10 9 8 7 6 5 4 3 2 1

Library of Congress Cataloging-in-Publication Data

Leckey, Andrew.
    The Morningstar approach to investing : wiring into the mutual
fund revolution / Andrew Leckey.
        p. cm.
    Includes index.
    ISBN 0-446-52013-6
    1. Morningstar, Inc.—History. 2. Mutual funds. I. Title.
HG4530.L38 1997
332.63'27—dc20   96-18170
                                                    CIP

Book design and composition by L&G McRee

To Matthew Leckey

Contents

■

FOREWORD

■

The small investor has few enough friends in the hustling world of modern finance, so it's nice to have Don Phillips and his Morningstar associates so brilliantly on the team. It's doubly nice to read, in the pages of this book, that our own concern for taking the individual seriously on *Wall $treet Week with Louis Rukeyser,* over national television for the past quarter-century-plus, helped inspire Don in what has become one of the most extraordinary and useful careers in the entire world of money.

Don is so gracious and modest a fellow that the straight-shooting thinking behind his amiable demeanor sometimes gets less attention than the formidable numbers he and his organization produce. I recall, for example, the first of his five appearances as my guest on television, in 1992 on our annual one-hour PBS special called "Louis Rukeyser's Money Guide," when I questioned him about what must have been a sensitive subject for a fellow trying to sell a mutual fund service. "My own thought has always been that investors shouldn't make an either/or choice between mutual funds and stocks," I said, "but what's your feeling?"

Don didn't hesitate for a second—even though much of the hype at that time was that funds replaced the need for (and were inherently superior to) stocks. "I agree with you entirely," he replied, adding that while mutual funds "have some advantages over stocks," this "by no means" meant that fund investors should not also invest in individual stocks. And when I pressed him as to whether he personally found it helpful to buy stocks as well as funds, he answered with a strong and unhedged "yes, I do," observing that anyone with his interests, and doing his kind of research, would find it "just natural" to "come up with ideas about stocks that you would want to pursue." Not exactly what the either/or headlines were screaming at the time, but sound common sense for many investors. For those with an interest in the subject, two piles—one for the professionals to manage, one for you yourself—have long been an ideal solution.

As Morningstar's fame and influence grew, so did Don's income—but not his ego. While others (notably the marketers of favored funds) made a religion on his "5-star" ratings, Don was quick to emphasize that, like such other ratings systems as The Rukeyser 100 in my own monthly newsletter, *Louis Rukeyser's Mutual Funds*, the star system is historical rather than predictive. "I don't own exclusively five-star funds," he confessed to me on television in 1993, agreeing totally that the star ratings were simply intended to be "a starting point."

Don was also invariably straightforward not just in revealing his own investing habits but in dealing objectively with the industry that Morningstar was covering with such remarkable care, persistence—and success. "Don, you're a gifted monitor of the mutual fund industry, but you're not a flack for it," I told him once. "You've been outspoken about some of its failings. What are you critical of right now?"

"Well," he replied without even a hint of a gulp, "I've been very critical of the way some of the funds have been advertising themselves. I think it's very important that we send investors the message of what's a worst-case scenario for a fund—not just what's the best angle, but what can go wrong with it. I also think that it's very important that we have more disclosure on funds; I think it's terrific, some of the work that the SEC has done to step up to make it a more level playing field, and make sure that investors have the information they need to make an informed decision."

And when I dug in one more time—"What funds do you hate now?"—Don unhesitatingly condemned one set of unimaginative managers with mediocre performance: those who run "funds that sort of look and feel like the S&P 500 but have above-average fees." Amen to that!

Don and the gang at Morningstar have done a genuinely extraordinary job of revolutionizing the way we look at, and keep track of, the exploding world of mutual funds. Given that explosion, even an industry whose choices are as varied and whose utility is as flexible as mutual funds needs all the sensible and clear-eyed monitoring it can get. When it comes, as it does from Don Phillips and Morningstar, with competence, integrity, and a sense of perspective, every investor should shout, "Hooray!"

—LOUIS RUKEYSER

Acknowledgments

■

The idea for this book was hatched with my literary agent, Nat Sobel, during the 1994–95 academic year, which I spent as a fellow at the Freedom Forum Media Studies Center at Columbia University. Nat and I then met on a cold and blustery winter day in Chicago with the Morningstar triumverate of Joe Mansueto, Don Phillips, and John Rekenthaler for lunch at a restaurant near the Morningstar offices. At that time, the two of us presented the book idea to them. I was asking for access to Morningstar's offices, meetings, staff members, and historical data, as well as the opportunity to talk at length with Mansueto, Phillips, and Rekenthaler as I constructed the Morningstar history and investment philosophy in book form. Morningstar would have no control over the content of the book that I wrote or any final say on what could be used. As a result, considerable trust would be required;

thankfully they were able to draw upon the many years of our professional relationship.

Morningstar lived up to its end of the bargain. In particular, I'd like to thank Mansueto, Phillips, and Rekenthaler for tirelessly spending hundreds of hours talking with me about the firm and investing amid their many other responsibilities. Their input made the book's historical information, myth-breaking concepts, and investment points possible. Other Morningstar staff members were also helpful in the project, as I made my regular week-long visits over a number of months to Chicago to observe and pick everyone's brain.

Thanks to Morningstar's Natalie Andrus, Laura Lallos, and the other mutual fund analysts for letting me follow their research process and attend their meetings. Additional appreciation goes to Catherine Gillis Odelbo, Liz Michaels, Jennifer Strickland, Gregg Wolper, Heywood Kelley, Patrick Geddes, Jeff Kelley, Catherine Voss Sanders, Jim Raker, Rika Yoshida, Beven Desmond, Michael Wynne, Doug Piper, Jacqueline Ta, Don Pietranczyk, Kim Lofton, Jason Meyer, Hassan Muhammad, Pete Downes, and Chuck Carlson. Many of the results of various talks and observations could not, due to space limitations, be put in the book, though they greatly influenced its overall tone and direction. All performance data and charts used in this book were provided by Morningstar.

My editor at Warner Books, Rick Wolff, was enthusiastic and instrumental in putting together the final product, drawing upon his years of experience in financial publishing. He was also quite understanding, as I was completing the writing of the book amid my existing syndicated newspaper column writing and the start of my position as an anchor at the CNBC cable television network.

Acknowledgments

Many thanks to the Freedom Forum and its devotion to research on important media trends, which made this book about a cutting-edge investment publisher possible. Thanks go also to Nat Sobel for his determination and to Morningstar for its patience and accomplishments.

INTRODUCTION

■

It was more than a decade ago that I first made a point to get to know Morningstar personally, after noticing the tiny lettering "Morningstar-Chicago" as the attribution at the bottom of a mutual fund performance chart in *Business Week* magazine. It was an unknown company to those of us more used to seeing names of other research firms on published fund data in those days.

In fact, telephone directory assistance twice mistakenly gave me the number to the Morning Star Baptist Church on Chicago's South Side as I was calling to try to set up an initial interview. My first interview with a very young, baby-faced Don Phillips was held in the company's cramped, austere offices in the historic brownstone Monadnock Building in Chicago's business district. Phillips's own office, complete with yellowed and torn window shade, 1940s-style desk and chairs, and antiquated telephones, looked like it hadn't experienced any changes in decades of use by prior tenants. There was only a handful of employees on board at this early operation.

In giving me an understandably brief tour of the facilities, which included a few computers in stark, undecorated rooms, Don motioned to founder Joe Mansueto's similarly modest office. He made a brief introduction and Mansueto responded with a small wave and brief smile. "We've got some big plans," Phillips said with conviction as he shook my hand while I waited for the elevator. "Uh, yeah, I wish them the best," I thought to myself, unconvinced, as I rode down the building elevator to the dark lobby below.

Over the course of the next few years, I did more newspaper and television interviews at Morningstar. Each time, I saw more and more computers being hooked up and more and more new staffers being given their orientation. If sheer numbers were any indication, Morningstar, it seemed, did have some big plans under way. At the same time, more investors were following its information either through direct subscription or in the national and local media.

Morningstar is not the only mutual fund research firm that I consult during the course of my work. Besides its competitor Lipper Analytical Services, through my syndicated newspaper column I regularly confer with and quote more than a half-dozen mutual fund newsletters that I hold in high regard. There are, however, reasons why I decided to ask Morningstar for access to its offices, meetings, and staff members. I felt it had a unique corporate history, a distinctive approach to research, numerous accomplishments that have changed the fund industry, and plenty of worthwhile investor information that had never been compiled in book form. In addition, I myself was curious to learn more. Taking such an inside look would be helped by my vantage point of having covered the company from its earliest days.

On one occasion about seven years ago, I was doing a television interview with Phillips in his office. Since the yellowed window shade dominated the area behind his desk, my camera crew would generally roll it up all the way so it wouldn't be visible on air. An initial camera setup is always done to adjust lighting and get a sound check, so I always ask a warm-up question that won't be used on air. In this case, I asked him how the preceding year had been for mutual funds. "Actually, it was a pretty good year, although bond funds did much better than stock funds," he replied as the camera swiveled from the left to the right. Then we began the actual interview, which lasted about twenty minutes. The camera crew shot a few additional office scenes and we headed back to the television station.

Later that day, about fifteen minutes before airtime, the segment producer who was editing my story ran to my office door at the station, out of breath and with a stunned look on her face. "There's . . . there's . . . there's nothing on the tape," she said with a gasp of horror. It turns out that the crew was using a brand-new type of camera for the first time that day. After getting the initial setup shot on tape, the cameraman had mistakenly pushed the "off" button rather than the "record" button. Absolutely nothing else from the lengthy encounter had been taped.

Once I shook off my disbelief, I looked at the tape and decided we could still use the Phillips line that said, "Actually, it was a pretty good year, although bond funds did much better than stock funds," even though the shot did move a bit from one side to the other. I then raced back to my office to bang out some additional sentences of my own and threw in a few graphics and footage of mutual fund investors to fill out the segment. I telephoned Phillips to explain the mess, telling him that there was nothing wrong with his many other more thoughtful comments and that we certainly hadn't made a conscious effort to dump them.

"Really, Don, we do know that you know a whole lot

more than that single sentence indicates," I said, at a loss for much else to say. He was gracious about it all. And, as it turns out, Phillips and Morningstar did know much more than we were giving them credit for in those early days.

CHAPTER 1

■

A MORNINGSTAR DAY

---

*"Only that day dawns to which we are awake. There is
more day to dawn. The sun is but a morning-star."*
—FROM *Walden*, HENRY DAVID THOREAU

It's 6:30 A.M. and Bevin Desmond is headed for work.
Wearing T-shirt and shorts, she straps on her in-line skates
and clatters down two flights of stairs to the sidewalk in
front of her apartment on Chicago's North Side. There she
adjusts her wrist guards, steadies herself, takes a deep breath,
and begins gliding with long, purposeful strides down the
street, her long reddish blonde hair flowing behind her in
the wind.

Fifteen minutes later, she reaches the apartment of co-
worker Heath Deyo, his shoulder-length brown hair tied
loosely into a ponytail for the trek. Similarly clad in T-shirt
and shorts, he has protective knee pads as well. In a

moment, his skates are on and they're both on their way. With their destination firmly in mind, each has the day's work clothes stuffed into a backpack. They'll cruise one of two time-tested routes, depending on the Windy City weather and their moods. The first is six and a half miles down the scenic lakefront, bone-chillingly cold at times, to Michigan Avenue and then over to Wacker Drive. The second is five miles long, winding through scenic Lincoln Park past the zoo and then down La Salle Street, whose tall buildings provide shelter from the wind.

Their next-to-last stop is always the Starbucks coffee shop in the Merchandise Mart, where Heath tanks up on caffè latte, with an extra shot of espresso, to jump-start his day. Desmond, a twenty-nine-year-old recruitment coordinator, and Deyo, a thirty-year-old computer programming manager, are now ready to get down to business. They take off their blades, put on street shoes, and walk over the Chicago River bridge to a tall white office building at Franklin and Wacker, one of the city's windiest corners. Then it's up the elevator and through the large glass doors using their electronic pass cards for access. It's now almost 7:30 A.M. and Desmond and Deyo are ready to begin their workday.

They work at Morningstar, one of America's most-quoted investment research firms. It is not a conventional pin-striped think tank. It has its own unique approach to investing.

Morningstar has used technology to provide average mutual fund investors with sophisticated information previously available only to large institutions. It has been an advocate for both industry change and investor rights. In existence just thirteen years, the company has carved a niche within an industry that has exploded to 9,000 mutual funds flush with $3 trillion in assets. It accelerated the move toward no-load (no initial sales charge) funds by placing fee structures under greater scrutiny. Its research page for each individual mutual fund is credited with giving all funds a level playing field.

Step inside:

Employees can stop by its "Coyote Cafe"—named for a car-bumper metal sculpture by John Kearney that's located on the same fourth floor—for a free soda or cup of gourmet coffee. There are aquariums stocked with tropical fish. Started up in a small apartment, Morningstar now has a growing staff of 350. Its office space covering four floors of 25,000 square feet each at 225 West Wacker Drive is a place where casual attire consisting of workshirts or jeans is the rule, rather than strictly a Friday event. When the 401(k) retirement program Morningstar offers to its employees was profiled in a national newspaper, the article's focal point was a large photograph of goateed circulation manager Chuck Carlson in workshirt, jeans, and hiking boots sipping a tall cup of coffee.

The company sets no limits on either employee sick days or vacation time, gives new fathers and mothers eight weeks off with full pay, and grants six-week paid sabbaticals to those who have been with the company four years. It has "thirtysomething" top managers and "Generation X" staffers who work under a loose corporate structure. There are no individual offices, with small cubicles even for the top brass.

It is not bound by tradition. You might call it investment research with "an attitude."

Here are a few myths about mutual fund investing that were exploded by Morningstar research and will be discussed in this book:

- Competition and economies of scale from more mutual funds being made available are bringing down expenses that funds charge.
- A big mutual fund won't perform nearly as well as an agile small fund.
- Taxable bonds do a terrific job of preserving your capital.

- Index funds are always the best way to play the market.
- A fund's name and the goals stated in its prospectus accurately tell its story.
- Buy only no-load funds and never a load fund.
- Stay clear of riskier funds because historically they have the worst returns.
- Market timing is a shrewd way to make money with mutual funds.

It's worthwhile for the investor to learn how Morningstar came into being and goes about tracking funds, rating them as to performance and risk—often prompting controversy in the process—and comparing them to their peers. It produces ten print publications and a half-dozen electronic products on mutual funds, closed-end funds, variable annuities/life insurance products, and equities.

Leadership includes thirty-four-year-old president and chief executive Don Phillips, selected one of the nation's "Top 20 Market Movers" by a leading financial magazine; thirty-nine-year-old founder and chairman Joe Mansueto, who stepped out of daily involvement in the company in early 1996 to pursue other entrepreneurial ventures; and thirty-five-year-old publisher of managed products John Rekenthaler.

The company has an eclectic nature. Many of Morningstar's fund analysts favor the alternative rock music of bands such as Jane's Addiction or the Pixies. Its corporate name comes from the classic work by Henry David Thoreau that urges living life to the fullest, though in a simple and thrifty manner. Frugal billionaire investor Warren Buffett is a role model. Bill Gates's Microsoft Corp. provides a template for its casual but intensely focused campus-like environment. Finally, the slick Crate & Barrel housewares chain is an example of the marketing creativity to which it aspires.

Morningstar doesn't pull punches. This in-your-face

personality, sometimes a source of aggravation to portfolio managers, helped it gain attention quickly.

Here's the company's track record as it has wired into the mutual fund revolution:

• Its editorial "Lies, Damned Lies, and Fund Advertisements" on February 19, 1993, led to major changes in what was considered acceptable mutual fund advertising. It blasted advertisements of the Pilgrim fund family for inaccurately claiming it had the five top-performing funds overall among all funds. This stand ultimately led to new National Association of Securities Dealers regulations on ads.

• The company popularized the concept of "risk-to-reward" in analyzing mutual funds. This is an important first screen, especially when determining the best all-weather funds designed to achieve for the long haul. It's a concept that was accepted academically, but hadn't been a factor in the ranking of mutual funds. What does the Morningstar 5-star rating really mean? Is it a valuable gauge for individual investors to follow or a misleading consideration that's being blown out of proportion? That will be considered in detail.

• It was the first to publicly urge the Securities and Exchange Commission to require mutual funds to list portfolio managers of funds and the history of manager changes. It began calling for this in 1989, four years before the SEC mandated that fund companies provide such information. Morningstar had been running the names of those managers that it had been voluntarily given since 1984.

• It was the first to declare that, because stock mutual funds generally own the stocks of different companies than those represented in the Standard & Poor's 500, that index isn't a suitable gauge for comparison. The average stock fund includes smaller-capitalization, faster-growing stocks

5

than the S&P 500. As a result, in the late 1970s through early 1980s, the average stock fund did twice as well as the S&P 500. In some more recent periods in which larger stocks have shone, the S&P 500 has held the advantage. A better benchmark would be a variation of the Wilshire 4500, which is more small-capitalization and growth-oriented.

• It has made accurate calls on likely results of portfolio manager changes at the nation's largest stock mutual fund, Fidelity Magellan. While many had predicted certain doom for the fund, Morningstar maintained that it could continue to be above average, if not great, under each leadership change. It might not always be smooth sailing, but Fidelity would always make a point to select a top manager to steer its flagship.

• It was the first to grade shareholder reports of mutual funds, its list of fund companies with A grades also winding up to be the organizations with fine returns in the 1990s. It seems that you can sometimes judge a book by its cover. When Morningstar started grading funds, some companies said it would cost too much to attain the top standards. Ironically, the fund families with the worst grades had the highest fund expense ratios.

• It was the first to calculate and print the brokerage costs of funds, a hidden expense that isn't included in a fund's expense ratio. Most investors don't know that it's not included in other costs. It had to be dug out of each fund's statement of additional information in Part B of its prospectus. For example, the smallest brokerage costs, those of Vanguard index funds, are one-hundredth of a percent. Some others are as high as one to one and a half percent.

• It warned of potential dangers of adjustable-rate mortgage funds, short-term world income funds, a variety of "bad idea" bond funds, and emerging market funds before they actually ran into serious trouble. It pointed out that whenever the fund industry has stretched itself, it has gotten into serious trouble.

• It was the first to regularly track strategies such as derivatives, emerging markets, and private and illiquid securities in mutual funds. These can have dramatic impact on many funds when investors least expect it. Fund managers have in some cases done things to "prop up" returns, in the process changing the personality of some funds altogether. These attempts go unnoticed no longer, though some fund companies complain that investors should simply trust them to do the right thing rather than demand the specifics.

Whether you wish to characterize Morningstar as a New Age trendsetter or an irreverent group of whippersnappers, what counts in the end is the information and advice its research efforts can provide mutual fund investors.

CHAPTER 2

∎

RESTLESS HEARTS

"I'm not one to enjoy sitting in meetings. What I'm good at, and what I like, is the entrepreneurial side, going from nothing to more than $30 million in annual sales."
—JOE MANSUETO, MORNINGSTAR FOUNDER
AND CHAIRMAN, WHO STEPPED DOWN FROM
DAY-TO-DAY INVOLVEMENT IN THE FIRM IN
EARLY 1996

It was 1982 and twenty-four-year-old Joe Mansueto was, as he puts it, "dabbling" with his newly purchased IBM PC. As an investment analyst, he was frustrated by a lack of comparative information about mutual funds. There was nearly $300 billion in U.S. mutual fund assets at the time, but no source providing a detailed up-to-date picture of a fund to help investors make their own decisions. Maybe putting annual report and prospectus information into one central publication would be a start, he reasoned.

He sketched his rough concept of a mutual fund "sourcebook" using data he'd entered into his computer for one initial mutual fund. These early papers, pulled recently from his files, show the words "Acorn Fund" drawn with ballpoint pen in large one-inch-high letters with jagged decorative fill-in lines on either side, placed over the inscription "Aggressive Growth, No-Load Fund, Yield 3.2%." The typed-out "Investment Criteria" follows, along with "Performance Data" tracked on a graph using keyboard asterisks. A listing of the fund's portfolio holdings, directors, sales charges, dividends, address, and telephone numbers follow. Mansueto wanted to mold a business that was right in line with the no-frills professionalism of his investment heroes, Warren Buffett of Berkshire Hathaway and international fund guru John Templeton.

The name for his imaginary company of the future had come to him as a freshman at the University of Chicago in 1974 as he was reading Henry David Thoreau's *Walden*. As he read the last sentence, the word "morning-star" popped out at him. "To me, the last line is an optimistic statement that says even the sun, which has been around so long, is just getting started," said Mansueto, a soft-spoken fellow with neatly trimmed light brown hair and a wardrobe straight from The Gap, whose seriousness about the firm's goals sometimes takes on a near-religious tone.

Mansueto was always intent on becoming an entrepreneur—even as a youngster in Munster, Indiana, where he was one of four children of Mario Mansueto, a physician, and Sara, a nurse. "Joe was always turning a little profit, beginning with the $50 he made by selling the $100 ham radio equipment he owned for a year as a youngster," recalls his mother. At the University of Chicago, Joe and roommate Kurt Hanson turned their apartment into a snack service, with trucks delivering cases of cola and potato chips to be sold to fellow students. "There was never a moment in which Joe ever indicated he would go the regular job interview route with major corporations prior to graduation like his fellow MBA classmates," recalls Hanson. After graduation in 1980, Mansueto and Hanson started up a firm doing research for radio stations. Mansueto subsequently left for a job at a venture capital firm, then served a stint as a stock analyst. But he wanted to build something himself, not place bets on other people's companies.

Primary information on mutual funds in those days consisted of the annual Wiesenberger volume used by libraries and institutional advisors; publications and software by the CDA organization designed for brokers and financial planners; and Lipper Analytical Services' data for fund companies and institutions. (The combined CDA/Wiesenberger business is now owned by a Canadian publisher.) None were aimed specifically at the average investor.

In April of 1984, Mansueto took the plunge into his mutual fund publishing firm, though he had no management experience whatsoever.

This project was started in the one-bedroom apartment he was renting in a high-rise building at Clark and Wrightwood, right next to a McDonald's restaurant, on Chicago's North Side. He took all the furniture that was in his living room and shoved it in his bedroom, then bought two tables on which to set personal computers. His living room was now the office. His initial investment out of savings was $75,000. Next, he hired a couple of full-time staffers and a pair of part-timers. As soon as checks began rolling in from the *Mutual Fund Sourcebook* for equity funds (which made its debut in November 1984), Mansueto rented 650 square feet of office space in the renovated, but still somewhat dreary, Monadnock Building in the heart of Chicago's financial district. The company had $94,000 in sales its first full year and $155,000 the second year. After publishing the quarterly *Sourcebook* two years, the company

11

introduced the more frequent binder publication *Mutual Fund Values*, featuring the one-page analysis of funds that was to become the firm's cornerstone. It also added bond funds to its coverage.

The start-up of *Mutual Fund Values* (later renamed *Morningstar Mutual Funds*) required more capital. Ultimately, Mansueto put $250,000 into the venture and borrowed a like amount from his parents. Today, he has a little less than $500,000 invested in the firm and is its sole shareholder, though others have options to purchase shares. Annual sales have grown to $31 million, with a goal of a long-term 25 percent annual growth rate. So long as there are reinvestment opportunities for development of new products and services, however, an annual bottom line at the break-even point is considered acceptable.

The timing of computer advances played a role in the introduction of the *Mutual Fund Sourcebook*. No one really knew whether a PC was capable of producing something so ambitiously data-intensive. A 10 megabyte drive was considered enormous and a 20 megabyte drive was almost unheard of. When the publication pushed these marvels beyond their capacity, they'd often crash and disrupt work. Two years later, technology would help out again, through the introduction of Apple Computer's Macintosh. The company bought a Mac in 1986 for the production purpose of extracting mutual fund data from the IBM PC. The information was ported to the Mac, and desktop publishing was used to produce the pages that became *Morningstar Mutual Funds*. In 1986, the company officially took the name Morningstar Inc., with the intent of creating a family of financial information products. The firm's first $6,500 advertisement in *Barron's* resulted in $25,000 in paid subscriptions.

Opportunity knocked in November 1985 when *Business Week* magazine asked for a large chunk of data about mutual funds. *Business Week* assistant managing editor Paul Sturm had just joined the magazine from *Forbes* and decided to add a mutual fund issue. Mansueto expressed "unbridled enthusiasm" and traveled to New York to hammer out what information would be required. *Business Week* insisted upon a fund rating system, and development work on the magazine's rating system paved the way for Morningstar's own 5-star system that represents a fund's risk-adjusted performance record. The magazine's mutual fund issue came out February 26, 1986, about the same time Morningstar introduced its star system.

Mansueto's tiny staff had endured erratic computers and hundreds of follow-up telephone calls to fund companies. He had gone to dinner at the nearby Five-Way Chili restaurant near the office every night, then run back home to work on the *Business Week* project late into the night. But the issue gave Morningstar instant credibility. When it contacted portfolio managers, its mention often kept a manager from hanging up the telephone. Company sales went to $750,000 in its third year of operation, $1 million in its fourth, $2 million in its fifth, $4 million in its sixth, and $11 million in its seventh.

Don Phillips, who was to become Morningstar's chief public figure, was hired in the fall of 1986 after receiving his M.A. in English from the University of Chicago. Initially, he was the firm's sole writer and analyst. "I outlined the new publication and basically was in charge of the editorial content, which required first of all that I read 777 fund prospectuses and write investment criteria from them," said Phillips, a husky, affable man who always speaks in careful complete sentences and is equally comfortable wearing a casual pullover sweater or a dark business suit at the office. He was grinding out analyses on forty funds in each two-week cycle, phoning individual portfolio managers for interviews as well. Phillips was to leapfrog in the company hierarchy from analyst to editor, then from publisher to president. In recent years, he has delivered more than 100 speeches annually to investor groups around the country and still writes many commentary pieces for *Morningstar Mutual Funds*. When Mansueto stepped down from daily company involvement in early 1996 to research special projects such as Internet involvement and possible entrepreneurial ventures, Phillips formally took charge of running the company.

His fascination with investments began early. When he was a fourteen-year-old in Dallas, his father bought him shares of Templeton Growth Fund, and that initial investment was bolstered by proceeds from the youngster's paper route. His diversified portfolio grew throughout his high school and college years. His father, Don Phillips (the Morningstar president is Don Phillips II), who runs a venture capital firm, said his son at an early age was a "quick study" who'd calculate daily batting averages of Texas Rangers baseball players, in much the same manner he would one day number-crunch fund returns.

Sitting together watching *Wall $treet Week with Louis Rukeyser* on television each week was a top priority for father and son, and Rukeyser became a valued mentor. The younger Phillips recalls his rapt attention the evening Sir John Templeton, the man who ran *his fund*, was interviewed on the program. Rukeyser's basic concept of taking the individual investor seriously was gradually driven home, and would become a force in Phillips's own career. Later, as a mutual fund expert, he would have the thrill of being interviewed by Rukeyser on television five times and of appearing as an authority on that subject at the world's largest investment conference, held annually in Las Vegas for subscribers to the *Louis Rukeyser's Wall Street* and *Louis Rukeyser's Mutual Funds* newsletters.

Another main Morningstar player is John Rekenthaler, who'd known Phillips while both were graduate students at the University of Chicago. Rekenthaler completed his coursework for an M.A. in English after spending a year

14

working at IBM. "I got hired in February 1988 because the stock market crash of the prior year meant investors were seeking more information about their portfolios and that translated to more jobs at Morningstar," Rekenthaler recalls. He spent his first three years as a fund analyst before becoming editor of *Morningstar Mutual Funds*. Known for his pithy, intense commentaries, he was named publisher of managed products with control over editorial content in 1995.

Wearing a suit and tie to work each day even though there is no company dress code, Rekenthaler is the office roadrunner, going full-speed toward another meeting or telephone call. Unlike those of Phillips, Rekenthaler's investment research accomplishments fulfill no family expectations. In fact, his mother, retired schoolteacher Donna Rice, sighs that there were "no real capitalists in our family before," and had hoped John would grow up to be a lawyer for an environmental or civil rights group.

As in most start-up companies, early staffing was small and the work week long. Another influential analyst in that formative period was Catherine Gillis Odelbo, who became convinced of the need for comparative mutual fund research when she was working in her father's financial planning business. Liz Michaels, hired from another investment research firm, coordinated the company's aggressive moves into CD-ROM, floppy disks, and most recently the Principia and Ascend products for Windows technology. Odelbo is now publisher of Morningstar Equities Group and Michaels is publisher for electronic products.

Publications tracking variable annuity/life insurance performance and closed-end funds were added to the product mix in 1991. International stocks and equities were to follow. Print and electronic products are offered for all the investments, with the exception of equities, which is strictly electronic. In late 1993, Morningstar moved into leased space in a newer building at 225 West Wacker. While its largest-circulation products are the *Morningstar Investor* newsletter and the mutual fund binder products, its electronic products, which allow greater direct comparison of individual investments, should grow at a much faster clip. Phillips expects the company in the future will sell basic software, while offering constant on-line updates delivering fresh data.

Every Morningstar mutual fund analyst responding to a questionnaire said that electronic products will likely lead the way in the future. But several added that any investment publisher is only as good as the data it gathers and conclusions it draws. Even in the era of cyberspace, the bells and whistles had better not be the main attraction.

CHAPTER 3

■

EXPLODING MYTHS

"We turned the keys of our Morningstar database over to individuals and said, 'Take it for a spin, do whatever you want.' We also set out to systematically break down any generally accepted concepts in the fund industry that we didn't believe were necessarily true."
—DON PHILLIPS, MORNINGSTAR PRESIDENT

The mutual fund mythmaking machine has been running full blast for more than a decade. It's time to pull the plug.

The skyrocketing rise of mutual funds has bombarded investors with an endless array of plausible, yet often ill-founded, beliefs about funds and how they operate. What makes sense to the uninitiated often turns out to be incorrect. To shoot down many of the generally accepted myths surrounding the industry, Morningstar has focused a combination of research and common sense on misunderstood concepts such as expenses, risk, disclosure, performance, and fund managers. Since Morningstar has been in existence about thirteen years and is decidedly youthful in its approach, it's not mired in the homilies of the past. Once investor heads are cleared of all the unnecessary noise, it believes, they can focus realistically on important issues at hand.

One place you'll encounter stark realists is the two-day Morningstar Mutual Funds Conference, held each spring with more than 400 investors, financial professionals, and financial journalists from around the country in attendance. They've done their homework.

"Let's take the next question," Jeff Kelley, senior editor of the *Morningstar Investor* newsletter, said into the lectern microphone at the dais in the giant ballroom of the Chicago Downtown Marriott at one conference. He motioned toward a gray-haired man seated at a back table who was waving his hand for attention.

A young Morningstar staffer carried a handheld microphone back to the chap wearing a tweed sports jacket, who might have either been an investor or planner, but most definitely was nobody's fool. He began to carefully pose his query to Lawrence Auriana, co-manager of the high-flying Kaufmann Fund and one of the three members of an august panel on aggressive equity funds.

Would he ask celebrated manager Auriana how he put together such an impressive track record? Did he wonder which small-company growth stocks would perform best in coming months?

No, Morningstar followers aren't fund groupies. They get right to the bottom line.

"Mr. Auriana, why is it that the expenses of your fund are among the highest in the industry?" the gentleman asked in an accusatory tone.

Pause. Heads throughout the room nodding in agreement. A few smirks. Several members of the audience craning their necks to get a better look at the interrogator. These folks weren't rubes; they all knew the *truth* about expenses and how they can hamstring mutual fund returns.

"Yes, it is true that we have one of the higher expense ratios," Auriana responded coolly as he locked the questioner in his gaze, acknowledging the hefty 2.29 percent annual expense ratio that *MMF* points out in every analysis it does of the Kaufmann Fund. "But we feel that those who invest with us do get their money's worth."

Many investors in this relatively new industry have culled much of their knowledge from articles extolling "The *Only* 10 Funds You'll Ever Need," aggressive advertisements, sales pitches from representatives of financial firms, and the advice of well-meaning friends or relatives. Less savvy folks want desperately to believe all the hype that declares the fund they're about to purchase is almost magical, a product of geniuses, and likely to prosper no matter what future economic and market scenarios may bring. On the flip side of that investment coin, however, you'll find a typical Morningstar subscriber who knows the score.

Two dozen speakers, mostly fund managers, address the conference group. They not only talk, but also receive an earful from a sophisticated audience. Getting the opportunity to pick the brains of managers Elizabeth Bramwell of the Bramwell Growth Fund, Ronald Ognar of the Strong Growth Fund, Roger Honour of the Montgomery Growth Fund, or Auriana about their winning techniques is a rare opportunity. In addition, thirty exhibitors from fund companies or software firms display their wares on long tables in the hallway outside the conference rooms. About twenty assigned Morningstar employees staff the conference by performing every task from handing out materials to checking coats. Another 150 introduce speakers, sit in on sessions, or talk with fund managers in order to get the latest scoop on fund trends. Those in attendance want answers that have a bearing on the prospects of their own hard-earned money or that of their clients. So don't patronize them. Tell them something new or don't waste their time.

It pays to pay attention when Morningstar explodes myths about mutual funds. Not just so you can be a know-it-all at your next cocktail party, but because it is, after all, your money. Following are myths of particular interest to average investors and financial professionals alike that Morningstar seeks to explode.

Myth No. 1: Thanks to the competition and economies of scale generated from more and more mutual funds being made available, the expenses that funds charge are declining.

Industrywide expenses are actually rising, Morningstar has unfortunately found. The various forms that these expenses take are constantly changing as fund companies attempt to make them less visible.

Fund companies are incredibly profitable because they have the ability to charge so many fees. In fact, were their fees cut in half, they'd still make money. Different funds have different sorts of ongoing annual expense structures, ranging from the extremely low one-tenth of 1 percent for a Vanguard Group index fund to a hefty 2.5 percent or more for the more costly funds of some other firms. A variety of loads are charged to get in and out of funds. What one would expect to be growing economies of scale from the introduction of so many new funds isn't working its way into mutual fund expense ratios. Today's fund investors are charged an average of $99 a year for each $10,000 invested in mutual funds, up from $71 in 1980, according to research conducted by Morningstar. Add to that three-tenths of 1 percent in commissions for the average stock fund, or even more in the case of active funds that run up hefty trading costs. Keep in mind that brokerage costs aren't included in the expense ratio, but are above and beyond it. Morningstar was the first to take this dollar amount and recast it in a form similar to the expense ratio.

For each 1 percent less in fees that an investor pays, he earns an additional 1 percent risk-free on his portfolio each year. It has become downright complex as Morningstar tracks the ongoing increase in expenses, however. Many funds have dropped or cut their up-front loads in recent years, instead charging less obvious higher annual fees. High fund expenses take an even more noticeable and painful bite in periods when fund returns are lower, a good reason why they're a crucial consideration whenever buying funds. There's a raft of fees, among them 12b-1 marketing fees, management fees, custodian fees, transfer-agency fees, shareholder servicing fees, accounting fees, administrative fees, legal and audit fees, reporting fees, insurance fees, and even printing and postage fees.

Stock funds charge 1.35 percent on average, meaning that you pay annual fees of $135 for each $10,000 invested in the average stock fund. Meanwhile, taxable bond funds charge 0.97 percent on average, or $97 for each $10,000 in an account, Morningstar has found. As a result of all these add-ons, investors annually pay more than $20 billion in annual fees on stock and bond funds. While an increasing number of discount brokerage services permit investors to select from hundreds of mutual funds without exacting a load or transaction fee, the three largest no-fee supermarkets charge at least 50 percent more than do other funds. It obviously makes sense to select from among the lowest-cost funds that they offer. You might even decide to pay the firm a trading fee to purchase low-cost funds that are not available as no-transaction-fee choices. It's a good idea for any mutual fund owner to sit down annually to compute exactly how many dollars you've paid. Those fees are very quiet killers.

Myth No. 2: A big mutual fund won't perform nearly as well as an agile small fund.

The fact that this statement about small funds being better than big funds has been made over and over doesn't make it true, Morningstar has found in its research. Furthermore, longer-term tax benefits accrue to investors in popular large funds that continue to gain assets.

It has taken a while for there to be enough evidence for the gigantic funds to demonstrate that they could keep on rolling up good returns despite their size, but enough results have now been turned in that this myth deserves to die. Fidelity Magellan, the largest of the large, is the most spectacular example of success, but there are many other large funds that continue to have good returns. They do not all simply replicate a market index, as critics had charged they would be forced to do because of their size, but are able to forge their own distinct investment personalities. Any performance disadvantage is a very minor one. Their portfolios may not be able to turn on a dime like some smaller funds, but managing them has not turned out to be an unwieldy, overwhelming feat either. Computers can do wonders in minding a large portfolio. It's also true that any smart fund company is likely to assign a top-flight manager to any fund that represents a major chunk of its overall asset base.

There can be a significant tax advantage to buying a popular large fund that continues to grow due to an influx of new shareholder money. All the new people who become shareholders serve to dilute the tax liability of long-time shareholders. They're shouldering the burden of the tax liability developed in the fund. So being a shareholder in a brand-name fund that's still growing is a definite boom tax-wise. Rapidly growing smaller funds would also be impacted by this, but their future growth rate is harder to gauge because they do not have the same track record of the larger funds.

Myth No. 3: Taxable bond funds do a terrific job of preserving your capital.

They don't preserve capital as they should because they pay out every penny in yield. Morningstar studies have found that taxable bond funds actually erode capital because they buy bonds at a premium price and the price of the bond subsequently declines to face value. The funds should have put some of that yield in reserve to make up for the decline.

In addition, because some bond funds dip into capital when paying these distributions, investors may find themselves cashing out their shares at much lower levels than those at which they originally invested. This is due to a combination of marketing pressures, accounting leeway, and poor disclosure. The first two factors explain why and how funds stretch their income, while the third indicates why they continue to do so without creating a scandal. Examining five- and eight-year time periods in which most interest rates declined a bit from start to finish, Morningstar found some painful results.

Assuming that investors spent their income distributions but reinvested their capital gains distributions into new shares, taxable bond funds as a whole lost about 1 percent annually during each of the two study periods. The worst offenders fell at more than twice that rate. The real problem is fund marketing, since too many taxable bond funds are sold strictly on yield. Rather than attempt to convince investors that bond funds are different from certificates of deposit, many fund companies continue to sell by emphasizing their funds' yield advantage over cash and downplaying issues of changes in principal. This leads to fierce competition among companies to post the highest possible payouts. Meanwhile, the raft of questions relating to distribution accounting, such as amortization schedules, prepayment, and other mortgage issues, and currency changes, too often permit the use of alternative accounting treatments. Funds choose these solutions that increase current distributions rather than others which would aid future capital.

Myth No. 4: Yield is one of the most reliable factors in considering taxable bond funds.

Yield is one of the least reliable factors of all, since any fund can play the high-yield game by buying securities with a high yield and employing accounting tactics to enhance the results.

On the other hand, not every taxable bond fund can make money for you over the long run by providing a solid total return, Morningstar studies have found. In years such as 1989, the group of high-yield funds with the very highest yields were the ones that lost the most money for investors. What yield does accurately indicate is the degree of risk taken in a fund. Most investors are looking for security and income in their bond investments. After all, if they didn't have security as their primary emphasis, they'd probably have bought stock funds instead. High yield isn't security; it's insecurity, Morningstar has found.

Myth No. 5: Mutual fund managers don't really add value to the money you invest because they don't have the skills to outperform the overall market.

This smug assertion overlooks some of the fundamentals of mutual funds, for it is not simply a case of mutual fund portfolio managers being "dumb and dumber," as some critics maintain. It is a more complex issue that must consider the particular benchmarks to which a manager's performance is being compared, as well as some of the costs inherent in managing funds.

Morningstar has found that there are definite reasons why funds underperform the market, other than the frequently offered beliefs that managers are simply (1) inexperienced,

(2) hyperactive traders, or (3) lacking in originality. Proving the value of fund managers is a complicated task, however. The easiest way to substantiate that money managers add value would seemingly be to look at growth funds and compare them against the Standard & Poor's 500, but that unfortunately gives you different evidence at different times. In the late 1970s, mutual fund portfolio managers routinely outperformed the S&P, so they were thought to be extremely smart. In the 1980s, especially the second half of the decade, they underperformed the index and therefore were thought to be quite dumb. From 1991 through 1993, they outperformed the index and were smart again, but then quickly slipped back to apparent stupidity. There were no particular comets shooting through the sky during those various periods to affect anyone's mental capacity, so other factors had to be considered by Morningstar in this performance question.

The fact is, over time the average mutual fund manager will slightly underperform the S&P 500 because of the constant drag of expenses, cash, transaction costs, and brokerage fees on the fund, Morningstar has found. This drag on results probably amounts to about 1.50 to 2 percent on a fund's return, though funds generally won't underperform by that full amount. Fund managers are professionals and better-informed than most people, so, on average, they add about one-half to 1 percent in value to a fund. Of course, some managers add a great deal more than that, a fact that savvy fund investors already know. That's obviously why they try hard to find the very best fund managers to run their money.

While most portfolio managers are indeed intelligent, there sadly are some shysters in the business, Morningstar has found. The more questionable examples aren't so much people hired by the bigger fund companies, but rather some of the more entrepreneurial people that may have started up a fund from very small beginnings. While many of these folks are upright and bright individuals, others are crooked and not very bright at all. Portfolio managers at some outfits are rewarded more for their marketing and speeches than for their ability to capably run funds. When a portfolio manager gives the impression that he believes he's smarter than everyone else, it's time to look carefully at his record to see how good his results really are. That counts more than a lot of bluster.

Myth No. 6: The beauty of mutual funds is that they simplify the investment process because they aren't really all that complex.

They aren't so simple that you should view them in a simpleminded manner.

Never underestimate the complexity of the investing process and overlook the fact that these are sophisticated modern financial instruments, not cleverly packaged answers to all of your investment prayers. Morningstar emphasizes that mutual fund investing is not a trivial pursuit. Funds are securities like any other security in that they have financial statements. They're also companies like any investment company and operate as such. Effectively tracking them, following their performance, and selecting them does take work on the part of the investor. Many factors must be considered. It's not so simple as picking the fund that seems to have a good track record. As in individual stocks, one shouldn't just pick a stock because it has shown it is capable of going up a lot, but should examine all facets of its potential. Funds are easier than stocks overall, in the sense that if you make a mistake it is less likely to be harmful. That's because funds, unlike individual companies, don't go bankrupt.

Myth No. 7: Index funds, whose stock portfolios match that of a broad-based index in order to mirror the overall market, are the best way to play the market.

They have their purpose, but espousing them alone is a big mistake. Morningstar research has found that they aren't the best choice in all cases.

Historical performance studies show that index funds tend to work best with more efficient, liquid markets such as blue-chip stocks, European stocks, and investment-grade bonds. The concept of index funds has been made considerably more worthwhile thanks to the trend of actively managed funds to boost their expenses. Yet the less the expenses of an actively managed fund, the less material advantage that indexing will have over it. If you have to make up for 2 percent in expenses each year when running a blue-chip stock fund that's competing with the S&P 500, you have to be remarkably good to beat the average by 2 percent a year. Index funds with tiny annual expenses each year, such as those of Vanguard Group, don't have to work so hard. Morningstar studies have found that indexing excels for blue-chip investing in basic large American multinational companies because so much is known about these firms that it's hard for active managers to add any value to them anyway. Many of the larger growth and income stock funds these days don't want to stick their necks out and take risks, so they wind up being very much like an index, except with expenses and cash holdings in the equation. They're still basically charging you for doing the same thing as an index fund. Few regular large-capitalization stock funds have enjoyed consistent success, with only a small portion beating the S&P 500 index over the past decade.

The good sense of index funds breaks down a bit when it comes to emerging markets indexes because there's usually an underlying question as to how a particular index has been constructed. Funds in less popular markets may thrive through astute management, offering their shareholders relatively attractive risk/reward profiles even if a few extra pennies are spent. Small-company stocks, junk bonds, and convertible bonds all fit into this category. As a result, you should skip the index funds in those categories, pay much less attention to various loads and other costs, and concentrate on the track records of the funds. The whole concept behind investing in a little-known market is to be the first clever buyer at the party, and also, presumably, the first at the bank.

Investing in an index fund doesn't mean that you don't believe that some active manager could do better. It means, rather, that you're content to give up your chance to allow an active manager to do so, so that you can receive a performance with a greater degree of predictability relative to the market and less impacted by fees. You also don't have to monitor what the portfolio manager is doing because he's basically on automatic pilot, the computers doing much of the work for him. The argument against indexing is that you can find managers higher on the talent curve with truly unique abilities that will outperform, rather than underperform, the market. That's true, but you need, however, to find someone who can beat the index over an extended period of time. Otherwise, it's not worth your effort.

These increasingly popular index funds are, by nature, a neutral tactic that consists of buying everything: the good, the bad, and the ugly. Assuming that stock returns follow a bell-curve distribution, an index fund will trail exactly half the stocks that make up its underlying index and beat the other half—a decent but scarcely enviable showing. Index funds are easy to use because shareholders truly control their own investments in that they don't have to commit money to managers who may or may not adhere to their prior investment tactics in the future. Best of all, index

funds are cheap. Still, they're not the answer to all investment needs.

Myth No. 8: It makes sense for an individual to own as many quality mutual funds as possible. The more, the merrier.

Sometimes enough is enough. Once you own more than a
half-dozen funds, you begin overlapping their goals,
Morningstar research shows.

If you buy seven funds, that last one is doing a lot of
the things that the first six funds are doing. Always ask,
"Is this fund doing anything differently than other funds
I own?" Rather than thinking about buying as many
funds as possible, think about how they fit together and
how their overall quality stacks up. I was once approached
by an investor who boasted of his large portfolio of different mutual funds. Amazingly, he had invested in more
than fifty funds in relatively small increments. If someone
is able to keep up with all of those funds and remain
knowledgeable about them, it obviously is one's preroga-
tive to do so. But for the most part it's not a great idea,
since a basic reason behind buying mutual funds is to simplify one's holdings. If you don't want to become confused with a great number of individual stocks and bonds,
you shouldn't be confused with too many funds either.

Worst of all, many investors hold a crazy-quilt array of
funds because every time they see an article about the top
funds, at the time they feel they must buy them all. Many
investors will buy popular funds that really don't meet their
goals, personal philosophy, or tax situation at all, or which
actually work against their other holdings. Running out to
buy the latest car model or designer fashion may be fine for
some people, but it makes absolutely no sense in your personal investments. Your investing shouldn't be tied to fads.

Myth No. 9: To invest efficiently, the costs associated with front-end loads should rank as your foremost concern.

That's putting the cart before the horse. A fund's annual expense ratio is considerably more important than the up-front fees that people examine most closely, Morningstar has determined.

Furthermore, the longer you hold a fund, the less concerned you should be with up-front charges and the more concerned with the annual expense ratio. Taking a $10,000 investment growing at a 10 percent annual rate for ten years, Morningstar tracked three different expense ratios. Its results found a dramatic difference among the results. Theoretically, a fund with no fees or expenses would've grown to $25,937, or a 150 percent gain. Using a .30 percent expense ratio typical of Vanguard index funds, you'll pay $698 over that ten-year period. With the 1.20 percent expense ratio typical of the average stock fund, you'll pay $2,694. With a 2 percent expense ratio that you'll find in more costly stock funds, your payout will be a much larger $4,348.

Of course, the very worst-case scenario is a fund with an up-front sales charge and a 2 percent expense ratio as well. In some cases, it might even be worth paying a sales charge for a fund that has a low expense ratio. Even if you paid 7.50 percent to get into a fund that earned 10 percent annually over a decade with .30 percent expenses, your investment would grow to $23,346. If you got into a no-load fund with 1.20 percent expenses that was growing at the same rate, your investment would grow to $23,243, or $103 less. The expense ratio, which can be obtained from the prospectus, is a factor worthy of more attention from investors. The amount of an expense ratio may seem small and its relation to other funds' expense ratios insignificant, but over a decade it can make a substantial difference. A high expense fund, all things being equal, will always be at a disadvantage.

One of the reasons why the money management business is so attractive is that the industry is compensated in such a seamless fashion. Consider 1994, in which the majority of mutual funds lost money, yet fund companies continued to collect their management fees. If, at the end of that losing year, investors had gotten a bill for money management of $2,000, there would have been a revolt, Morningstar believes.

Myth No. 10: Regulatory agencies such as the Securities and Exchange Commission make sure that the mutual funds we invest in are safe.

No agency can be everywhere. The SEC does a good job, but it can't make sure that funds are safe, Morningstar believes.

Regulators are like auditors in that there's just so much that they can do. They can monitor the overall process and try to root out fraud, but they really get to analyze an individual fund company in depth only about every seven years, Morningstar found. They can't stop funds from doing misleading things altogether or just offering dumb investments. Consider this: A particular fund might not break any SEC rules, the SEC may have given it a completely clean bill of health, and it may have been bought by an investor because he considered it to be quite safe. Yet it could still lose 40 percent in value for that investor in a calendar year without breaking any laws. Have confidence in regulators, but take the responsibility for your investments yourself.

Myth No. 11: Comments from portfolio managers give a clear indication of a fund's workings, since it obviously makes sense to go right to the horse's mouth.

Dream on. Not that portfolio managers are trying to deceive, but their minds can play tricks on them because they're so actively involved in managing their funds and dealing with such a raft of information.

Frequently, a manager will tell Morningstar analysts that he didn't have a security in his portfolio on a specific date, but checking the shareholder report indicates he actually did. If you as an individual investor have gone through a fund's shareholder report item by item, you're doing something the portfolio manager probably didn't do. In one instance, *Morningstar Mutual Funds* editor Catherine Voss Sanders had to listen to an irate portfolio manager lecture her on an aspect of fund accounting that involved an income distribution. He told her that if she didn't know this rudimentary fund accounting, she shouldn't be in the business of evaluating funds and should get a new career. She immediately telephoned the fund company's chief accountant and found out she was right and the fund manager was incorrect. In fact, there's a lot of fund accounting that fund managers don't know because it isn't germane to their everyday job of selecting securities. More than a few portfolio managers aren't up on tax issues, and really don't know what their distributions were last year. While there's a general assumption that portfolio managers are the ones in control, some items are more important to them than others. In addition, they make mistakes just like anyone else does.

Further complicating matters, Morningstar has found that fund managers also use language in different ways. They may say they're growth stock managers, but they define growth stocks very differently than other managers do. They may say they own blue-chip stocks, but they define the concept of blue chip very differently. Such terms that do not have quantitative definitions attached to them are used freely and in different ways. Morningstar sometimes has sub-scribers complain that a manager said something one way, but Morningstar said it another way. Neither party may be wrong, but each could be using the same terminology in different ways. Those definitions and the context must be defined.

Portfolio managers also typically love to talk to Morningstar analysts about their winners, but not their losers. They are, after all, human. If you confer with a fund manager whose portfolio was down 20 percent last year, all he'll want to do is chat about those few stocks that made money. His presentation is so positive that it almost makes you wonder how he managed to lose so much money in the first place. Of course, managers, like anyone else, like to present their best side. A stock name that's admired on Wall Street sounds a lot better in a conversation than one that nobody has heard about or that's been a terrible performer. Of course, it's also worth keeping in mind that a portfolio manager is hardly an unbiased source about his fund. Which means you really can't treat the words of portfolio managers as gospel.

Myth No. 12: A fund's name and the goals stated in its prospectus accurately tell its story.

If that were true, there wouldn't be much of a plot to the story. The names of many funds sound similar and like-minded, based upon attractive-sounding concepts that mar-keters know will sell, yet they operate with significantly different strategies than their generic names would imply. Morningstar has learned to take those names and stated goals with a grain of salt.

In some cases, a new manager may come on board and the fund's existing name and stated goals become only very loose concepts that aren't really followed. The entire complexion of that fund's inner workings may be changed entirely without a public acknowledgment of that occurrence. In some cases, a fund's stated goals actually permit more leeway and diversity than the portfolio manager actually intends to use in daily practice. They serve as more of a flexibility option for emergencies or a dramatic change in market conditions than as an accurate statement of how the fund will be run.

As serious-sounding and earnest as the stated goals of funds in their prospectuses may seem, don't take them literally. For example, most funds in the growth and income category state that their goal is to blend capital growth and income, yet they pay only a 2 or 3 percent yield. Clearly, if the goal was truly equal blending, they'd be getting a much higher yield than that. In practice, they expect to make 8 to 10 percent on growth and 2 or 3 percent on income. Morningstar has learned that what seems straightforward may not be at all straightforward in practice. Names and goals are untrustworthy as barometers. You're better advised to follow track records or to try to understand the philosophy of the portfolio manager running the fund.

Myth No. 13: The rest of the prospectus tells what the mutual fund is all about.

Only if you're a lawyer. The prospectus is a legal document written by lawyers for other lawyers to protect the fund from losses by sketching out a range of possibilities. That has not changed at all in the time that Morningstar has tracked them.

Such a document intended to protect a company from lawsuits has a decidedly different purpose from one designed to educate investors. You really can't educate about investments while thinking about potential loopholes at the same time. It is worthwhile to look at a prospectus of an investment you're considering, but keep in mind that you'll primarily be greeted by a bewildering gush of legalese.

Myth No. 14: A fund company's toll-free 800 number is a fast, excellent means of obtaining the low-down on a mutual fund's performance and how it operates.

This is sometimes an instance of getting exactly what you pay for. Don't be so sure that the representative you chat with on a fund company's toll-free number necessarily knows what he or she is talking about. Morningstar has found some of the information to be incomplete or incorrect.

These entry-level workers answering the telephone are much better equipped than they ever were before, more able to address questions because so much sophisticated information is computerized and at their fingertips. However, the data they access is often computed quite differently by different companies, making it difficult to compare apples to apples in many cases. Price/earnings ratios are a good example of that, depending on whether trailing twelve months or projected twelve months are being considered. There are also different conventions for handling items such as a loss in a fund.

Training of telephone personnel varies widely from firm to firm. Many companies lay these people off during downturns and then hire them back during boom periods. The individual you're speaking with may have joined the firm the very week you're talking with him, especially if it's a time of strong fund sales. Being given an inaccurate amount for the fund's cash position or mistaking $2 billion for $2 million isn't all that uncommon. I recall talking with the son of a television co-worker of mine, who explained to me that he had no financial background or interests whatsoever, yet got a first job out of college giving out information on the toll-free telephone of a large mutual fund company. He readily admitted that he didn't have a clue as to what he was doing and quite likely gave inaccurate information. This young fellow did, after a few months, exhibit the good judgment to quit the job and take up a new profession.

Morningstar regularly monitors fund companies' toll-free lines and has learned of their shortcomings. A classic incident occurred in 1994 when a Morningstar staffer asked about the duration of the bonds in a portfolio, to be told "seven years' duration, since the fund was started in 1987." Double-check the information or compare it to data from an outside source. There are different computations for different time periods of P/E ratios and market capitalizations, but responses should be in the same basic range, not skewed one way or another. If you do contact many of the fund firms whose staffers are well-briefed, consider yourself fortunate. Even then, don't go only on the information given in that phone call.

Myth No. 15: An investor should buy only no-load funds. Never buy a load fund.

Never say never. It depends in large part upon each investor's acumen at choosing funds and whether he wishes to pay for help.

To Morningstar's way of thinking, a sales charge is just one of many considerations an investor must evaluate in appraising a fund. Too great a weighting on this or any other single variable can cause an investor to neglect other considerations. For example, should investors have neglected Fidelity Magellan because of its 3 percent front-end load? Should Sir John Templeton's outstanding international funds have been rejected because of their loads? At the very least, an investor is clearly far better off in a good load fund than in a bad no-load fund. No longer is the fund industry divided along clear-cut lines with the full 8.5 percent load funds on one side and pure no-load funds on the other. In recent years, full-load groups have cut back their front-end sales charges, while formerly no-load groups have attached front-end loads to some of their funds. In addition, the popularity of deferred sales charges and 12b-1 fees has further clouded the distinction between load and no-load funds.

It's true that the performance after paying the sales charge tends to be less with a load fund, though in most cases that difference is money paid for information and service from a broker or financial professional. It can be money well-spent if you don't personally have the time, energy, or inclination to do your own research, and are receiving good advice from someone who knows what he's doing. You do not, however, want to pay that same charge to an uninformed salesperson.

Morningstar's underlying philosophy has been the empowerment of the informed individual investor willing to do his own homework, but if you'd rather dedicate yourself to other endeavors than selecting funds, you shouldn't be considered less than a complete person. For example, you're much better off if you learn to fix your own car. That way, if your brakes go out on the highway, you'll know what needs to be repaired, and you can be more self-sufficient. Other folks prefer to leave everything up to a reputable mechanic. With mutual funds, it needn't be a 100 percent deal, but instead a compromise in which the investor assumes some of the responsibility for selecting financial instruments, while ceding the rest to an investment professional. It's also not as though you can't find any good load funds, either. These days there are so many different mutual funds available that there are ample candidates for investment in both categories. Some highly successful portfolio managers work in both camps with separate funds, such as Shelby Davis with the load New York Venture fund and no-load Selected American Shares Fund. Both are winners. Morningstar's priority is to identify good funds, not to pass judgment on which distribution pattern is superior.

That said, Morningstar has discovered some differences in how load versus no-load funds are managed, particularly in fixed-income funds. More and more of the sales compensation of bond funds has been shifted to the expense ratio in the form of 12b-1 marketing fees. Those with high 12b-1 fees tend to take on considerably more risk than low-expense funds. Because the handicap of that expense ratio means total return and yield will be lower, many managers feel they must compensate by going into lower-credit-quality bonds or longer-duration issues that have much greater interest rate risk. This situation is most pronounced in short-term bond funds. Load funds traditionally have money market funds available on a no-load basis, in addition to their bond funds carrying a sales charge. Drawing the line between these two becomes difficult, for no investor will buy a money market with a load, yet no broker wants to sell it if it doesn't have a load that can provide him with a commission. A number of load organizations have responded by coming up with gimmicky products, such as short-term multi-market funds featuring a variety of bells and whistles designed to give an investor a slightly better yield than that of a money market return. These complex products have ultimately blown up on a lot of unwary investors. Clearly then, in short-term bond funds the no-load funds, by keeping their costs low and their strategies simple, have better served the investor.

Load fund families cause some of their own problems as far as their perception by investors. Many have blurred the investment process by issuing a number of different fund classes of the very same fund. In fact, more than half the new mutual funds introduced in the past two years have been merely repackaged versions of existing portfolios. There are typically A shares with a front-end load; B shares with a deferred sales charge; and either C or D shares, which are known as "level loads." Level-load fund fees pay the broker a flat 1 percent commission up front and a similar, or level, trailing commission for each subsequent year the investor holds the fund. This complicates matters and means investors, financial planners, and brokers waste valuable time pondering the structure rather than the real merit of the underlying investment. Instead of trying to shuffle and conceal the load through such hocus-pocus, load families would be better served to explain in a straightforward manner that the advice brokers provide with the funds make them worth the extra sales charge, Morningstar contends.

Myth No. 16: It makes sense to invest in mutual funds by carefully comparing the advertisements of the funds you're interested in.

This would be disaster. After all, would you buy your next car based strictly on the advice given to you in a car commercial?

Fund advertisements, while they are regulated to prevent the most egregious of misrepresentations, are advertisements and therefore designed to present a fund in the best possible light. Morningstar considers them snapshots that leave out a lot of information that's vital to the investor, such as what stocks the fund owns, an in-depth look at its track record, and a meaningful consideration of its risk. Mutual fund advertisements don't educate you; they entice you. They may pique your interest and get you started in your steps toward purchasing an investment, but that's about all they do.

Myth No. 17: Stay clear of riskier funds because historically they have the worst returns.

Risk is an important component of investing and you'll have to assume some of it if you are to obtain good returns. Riskier funds, Morningstar has found, do especially well coming out of market downturns.

Just as "no pain, no gain" is the philosophy behind rigorous physical training, a fund unwilling to assume any risk wouldn't achieve much. The judgmental tone taken by many toward higher-risk investments has created the false impression that assuming almost any form of risk-taking is a foolhardy activity. There actually are risks worth taking, and, in fact, there is actually considerable danger in remaining too timid. Low-risk status is a hollow victory if it's accompanied by paltry returns. Remember that risk avoidance is not an end unto itself. The opportunities to gain after a market downturn will be lost, and weak-to-mediocre investment returns will be assured. To the same extent that investors must resist the lure of top returns in giddy markets, the lure of perfect safety must be avoided in down periods.

If you're willing to assume risk at a market bottom, Morningstar studies have shown that it will pay off quite handsomely in the long run. View it as a buying opportunity. Concern about risk is often overemphasized, taking center stage following a period of downward market turbulence. In times of crisis and uncertainty, successful investors keep their sense of perspective. The connection between past risk and future risk in a fund is extremely powerful, considerably more potent than the connection between historical total returns and future returns. Whatever the market conditions, the riskiest funds have stayed the riskiest and the safest have stayed the safest. This makes risk a strong initial screen worth understanding fully.

To see how funds of various risk levels performed after

market downturns, Morningstar divided equity funds into low-risk, medium-risk, and high-risk categories and tracked them for three years following five different downturns. The findings were that after a downturn there's a strong tendency for higher-risk funds to outperform medium-risk, and for medium-risk to outperform low-risk.

The typical low-risk fund following those five down periods averaged a gain of 19.38 percent during the next twelve months, while the typical medium-risk fund was 22.95 percent, and the high-risk fund was a considerably better 25.70 percent. These three-year numbers reinforce the importance of staying in the market and being in aggressive funds. The low-risk return averaged 12.70 percent, medium risk 14.12 percent, and high-risk 16.03 percent. The results are just as dramatic for bond funds, which ran into trouble in the first half of 1987 and came on strong in late 1987 through 1988. If you get into a bond market after its bottom, you can make a lot of money. Ability to cope with higher-risk alternatives means a willingness to deal with some degree of volatility, which may or may not be your cup of tea. That is an individual decision.

Myth No. 18: If you select the right mutual funds and put together a solid personal portfolio, you can sit back without having to think much about them again.

Don't fall asleep at the wheel. Morningstar cautions investors to remember that funds change and people change.

You should check in on your funds annually, at the very least, to make sure that the portfolio managers and general investment processes remain in place and that performance and prospects are what you expect. Quarterly or monthly checkups would be reasonable for anyone who's somewhat more in tune with the financial markets or simply wants to be more active. If all isn't going the way you expected, find out the reasons why. If portfolios have taken turns you don't agree with, consider moving into different vehicles. One of the biggest investment mistakes that average individuals make is investing and then forgetting about their holdings. In today's fast-paced, computerized investment world, you must keep up with things or you'll be locked into yesterday's thinking.

Myth No. 19: Market timing is a shrewd way to make money with mutual funds if you're agile and can move quickly.

It's usually a dramatic way to lose money, and Morningstar has found that the records of market timers are nothing for anyone to be proud about. It's difficult to move intelligently within the market-timer's world of ambiguous or ill-fated telephone hotline messages and fax directives.

That's why the number of market-timer funds is dwindling and why these folks who make their money giving directives on fund switching are not held in the same high regard that they once were. No matter what the results, many devotees of these market-timers have a religious fervor to their faith in a particular timer that is unflappable even if results don't live up to expectations. Market-timers spend the vast majority of their time asking questions such as "Which way is the market heading?" Such an approach holds immediate appeal, since answers to that kind of question have obvious investment benefits. Unfortunately, in order to succeed, investors must ask not only those questions with the most valuable answers, but those that have the best chance of being answered correctly. To beat a market, one must know something that other investors do not. That's a difficult task when analyzing heavily scrutinized items such as interest rates or the market's near-term direction. Market-timers are always looking for the big score, such as a bull market call or the sidestepping of a severe bear market that serves to vault them to the top of the performance chart.

There can be better investment advice from analysts with a fundamental approach. They may, for example, discover a balance sheet irregularity or ask a corporate officer or supplier a question that other analysts have completely overlooked. Even though its successes are less dramatic, fundamental analysis holds greater potential for adding value than does market timing, Morningstar has determined. Such little advantages piled up consistently over time can create superior long-term returns, such as those realized by Sir John Templeton, Peter Lynch, and Warren Buffett.

Market timing will always be with us in some form or another, and seems to have a marked propensity for reincarnation. Perhaps that's because past failures are simply forgotten after a while. Market timing is nonetheless a marketer's dream, since the pool of investors seeking a shortcut to investment success is seemingly inexhaustible. Yet Morningstar has found that until even one timing fund can prove itself consistently in the real-world mutual fund setting, there's little reason for serious investors to pay heed to these systems. Of course, millions of people read the daily horoscopes as well. The difference, perhaps, is that horoscopes may just waste a little of your time, while market timing can waste a lot of your money.

Myth No. 20: There's no need to have a compelling argument for every single mutual fund that you own.

There'd better be, for if you don't know why you own a fund, you shouldn't own it in the first place. All investors should be committed to their holdings, Morningstar believes.

The first rule in investing is to fully understand all of your holdings, using the information you culled in studying the fund to form your own argument for owning it. In stock investing, former Magellan manager Peter Lynch has always urged investors to know why they're buying a particular stock based on reasons such as believing in the product it makes or expecting company sales to increase at a certain clip. Using the same philosophy, if you don't have an argument for why you bought a fund or why you should sell it, in effect what you've done is throw a dart. An investor must always have a game plan associated with a mutual fund choice. Too often investors almost impulsively throw together a portfolio based on publicized performance lists, advertisements, or an obscure advisor's recommendation. Their naïveté and detached attitude toward their holdings mean they're unlikely to monitor them properly and, more than likely, will hold them too long or sell them too soon.

Myth No. 21: International investing is often more trouble than it's worth, as proven by the tailspin some of the emerging markets have taken in the 1990s.

You can't judge any mutual fund group by any one- or three-year period. Morningstar has found that international stock mutual funds provide smart diversification for the typical U.S. investor who has most of his holdings in domestic stocks.

Of course, the investor should be aware that they will go through periods in which they significantly outperform or underperform the domestic market. For example, their returns were outstanding in the mid- to late 1980s, but they did poorly in the early 1990s. Emerging markets had been the exception by turning in strong performances, but a number of them plummeted. Morningstar advises that the average investor consider having as much as one-third of his assets in international funds, which is considerably more than most do now. It is true that the world's markets are more intertwined than in the past thanks to computers and international information, but there's still incredible uniqueness to each foreign country's stock offerings. International investing is useful as protection in case the U.S. market is going through a difficult period, but Morningstar advises that you should still have most of your assets in dollars because our liabilities are in dollars.

Myth No. 22: Go with a hot manager and you'll be rewarded with sizzling results.

A hot manager and his fund can also burn you. If you buy a fund based on the fact it was ranked number one over a one- to three-year period, Morningstar studies have found that you're more likely to obtain either extremely bad or extremely good results.

That's because a fund gets to be number one by following an extreme approach, and this should not necessarily be equated with genius. One might naively think that the only way to get to be number one is to be smart, but it more likely may indicate more a willingness to take chances. Even some conservative funds can wind up number one, but they may top the list simply because it was a three-year bear market and they had 80 percent in cash. The following three years, the market goes up and those same funds trail everybody.

Don't keep a personal portfolio with too many number ones in it, since they fit better on the edges of a portfolio. Emphasize funds with much more consistent performances, perhaps in the top quarter of the funds in its category but doing especially well for the long haul. The problem of putting number one on a pedestal is made worse by the fact that so many specialized lists of top performers are regularly printed in newspapers and magazines. This may be helpful information for people making decisions. But while it's not a recipe for disaster, it certainly isn't a recipe for success either. Great funds such as Vanguard Windsor have dry spells, but are worthy holdings over their long and noble history. The worst time to have bought Windsor was when it was number one, since at that point it was at the peak of its value. New England Value Fund is another excellent fund, but it had a two-year slump right after it ranked number one over a three-year period. At the point a fund is hot, it is probably overheating and about to cool down. Stay away until it looks more attractive from a price standpoint.

Myth No. 23: Mutual fund investing is serious business, not fun.

Economics is the dismal science, but investing certainly isn't. If you view your mutual funds with grim intensity, you'll keep up with them a lot less than you really should. Morningstar has made a business of making investment information as engaging, accessible, and comprehensive as possible.

We all learn a lot more when something interests us. It may not be as riveting as watching your favorite football team or the hottest new movie, but anything that seems like an adventure will soon become a top priority to you. We're all willing to spend enormous amounts of time on hobbies or activities such as constructing a house—so long as what we're doing isn't actually called work. The mutual fund business is constantly changing and investors must be diligent, yet many of the trends affecting the economy, stocks, bonds, and mutual funds are high drama worth following with enthusiasm. The boom in investment magazines, newspaper columns, and cable television programming indicate that a growing number of Americans consider investing to be great sport. It's a growing conversation topic everywhere you go these days as well, with fewer people willing to be considered a part of the investment illiterate. Mutual funds offer handy results and rankings through services such as Morningstar, and some devotees view these much like a horse race because one never knows exactly which individual funds, groups, or categories will win the short-term or long-term races. Mutual fund investing has a lot of numbers in it and therefore is deemed important, but, yes, it can truly be fun as well.

CHAPTER 4

■

THE PAGE

"Oh, mother, father, your blindness to our most blessed gift, nature, leaves us with the overwhelming task of correcting your utter mess."
—MESSAGE TO PARENTS IN THE LINER
NOTES OF COMPACT DISC "RITUAL DE
LO HABITUAL" BY ALTERNATIVE ROCK
GROUP JANE'S ADDICTION, THE MUSICAL
ARTISTS NAMED MOST OFTEN BY
MORNINGSTAR MUTUAL FUND ANALYSTS
IN A SURVEY AS THEIR FAVORITES

Putting together the data on more than 7,000 stock and bond mutual funds is a labor-intensive task that ultimately leads to formulation of "the page" in the Morningstar Mutual Funds binder.

"The page" is the Morningstar franchise and focal point

for its analysts. It's a jam-packed grouping of information in various little boxes that can be overwhelming at first glance. The "Analysis" section (Item 1 on the sample shown on page 52) is an overview that basically interprets and adds to the numerical data. A mutual fund analyst must write a convincing argument in 200 to 250 words based on performance data, potential, and historic risk, as well as relevant changes in a fund's tactics or operations. There are a lot of facts and suppositions to consider in putting together an analysis, just as there's a lot for average investors to consider when studying a Morningstar page.

Working the telephone takes up much of the day for the twenty or so MMF analysts who compose these arguments. They're setting up interviews with portfolio managers, conducting interviews, and poring over fund data. Each writes up about a dozen funds during a two-week publishing cycle, so that every mutual fund's page is rewritten every twenty weeks.

"You must have a strategy for trying to get through the page, and there are a number of different ways of going about it, so long as you keep in mind that selecting mutual funds is part science and part art," advised MMF contributing editor Catherine Voss Sanders, a journalism M.S. from Northwestern University whose wire-rimmed glasses and contemplative nature impart an intellectual air.

Whether or not an investor is a Morningstar subscriber or reader, the page's sections provide a good outline for what all investors should be scrutinizing when choosing their funds. Many of the most important sections are highlighted in this chapter and identified on the sample on page 52.

What, in capsule form, is the best quick path for the average investor through this page?

THE NICKEL TOUR

There's a favorite shortcut for investors pressed for time, according to Voss Sanders. Begin with each fund's historical returns and risk, then move on to examine its management team. Next, determine its performance year-by-year within its peer group, and then consider its risk in comparison to similar funds. Finally, check the style of the fund to see how it would fit into a portfolio of funds. Each investor, of course, must ultimately decide what's most important to him about a fund, but these are the recommendations of a professional analyst.

Start with the "Historical Profile" information box (Item 2 on the sample page) featuring separate information on return, risk, and star rating, which is located in the upper middle of the page. It includes the famous and sometimes infamous star rating, going from one star on up to five stars, which provides a snapshot of how the fund has performed historically on a risk–adjusted basis. This provides Morningstar's overall assessment of a fund's historical return and risk, and its overall risk–adjusted star rating. The return and risk assessments are based on a fund's historical performance relative to other funds in its broad investment category. The ten-year rating accounts for 50 percent of the overall rating, the five-year figure for 30 percent, and the three-year rating for 20 percent. The pros and cons of the 5-star rating system, which should only be a portion of what you look at, will be discussed at greater length in the next chapter.

Secondly, with all of the historical data on the page, it's crucial to consider whether the management team that built the fund's historical record is still in place. The "Portfolio Manager" biographical information (Item 3 on sample page) should be read early in the process to see whether other information will be relevant. It is rare to see a fund these days with a manager who has been there a decade; two to three years is much more common. With some funds, the portfolio manager has less impact than with others. Some have very set investment strictures, or operate

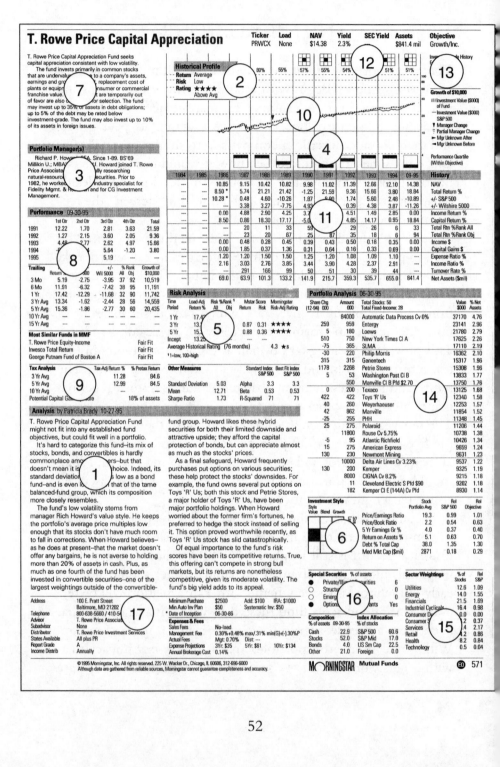

T. Rowe Price Capital Appreciation

Ticker	Load	NAV	Yield	SEC Yield	Assets	Objective
PRWCX	None	$14.38	2.3%		$841.4 mil	Growth/Inc.

T. Rowe Price Capital Appreciation Fund seeks capital appreciation consistent with low volatility. The fund invests primarily in common stocks that are undervalu— ... to a company's assets, earnings and gr— ... replacement cost of plants or equipm— ... nsumer or commercial franchise value. ...are temporarily out of favor are also c— ...for selection. The fund may invest up to 35% of assets in debt obligations; up to 5% of the debt may be rated below investment-grade. The fund may also invest up to 10% of its assets in foreign issues.

Portfolio Manager(s)

Richard P. Howa— CFA. Since 1-89. BS'69 Millikin U.; MBA ... U. Howard joined T. Rowe Price Associate ... lly researching natural-resource ...ecurities. Prior to 1982, he worked ...industry specialist for Fidelity Mgmt. & ... and for CG Investment Management.

Historical Profile
- Return Average
- Risk Low
- Rating ★★★★ Above Avg

Performance 09-30-95

	1st Qtr	2nd Qtr	3rd Qtr	4th Qtr	Total
1991	12.22	1.70	2.81	3.63	21.59
1992	1.27	2.15	3.60	2.05	9.36
1993	4.48	2.77	2.62	4.97	15.66
1994			5.64	-1.20	3.80
1995		5.19			

Trailing	Return	+/- Wil 5000	+/- All	% Rank Obj	Growth of $10,000
3 Mo	5.19	-2.75	-3.95	37 92	10,519
6 Mo	11.91	-6.32	-7.42	38 95	11,191
1 Yr	17.42	-12.29	-11.68	32 90	11,742
3 Yr Avg	13.34	-1.62	-2.44	28 56	14,559
5 Yr Avg	15.36	-1.86	-2.77	30 60	20,435
10 Yr Avg	—	—	—	—	—
15 Yr Avg	—	—	—	—	—

Most Similar Funds in MMF
T. Rowe Price Equity-Income	Fair Fit
Invesco Total Return	Fair Fit
George Putnam Fund of Boston A	Fair Fit

Tax Analysis
	Tax-Adj Return %	% Pretax Return
3 Yr Avg	11.28	84.6
5 Yr Avg	12.99	84.5
10 Yr Avg	—	—
Potential Capital Gain...	18% of assets	

Analysis by Patricia Brady 10-27-95

T. Rowe Price Capital Appreciation Fund might not fit into any established fund objectives, but could fit well in a portfolio.

It's hard to categorize this fund–its mix of stocks, bonds, and convertibles is hardly commonplace amo— ...ers–but that doesn't mean it is— ...hoice. Indeed, its standard deviation ...s low as a bond fund–and is even lo— ...that of the tame balanced-fund group, which its composition more closely resembles.

The fund's low volatility stems from manager Rich Howard's value style. He keeps the portfolio's average price multiples low enough that its stocks don't have much room to fall in corrections. When Howard believes– as he does at present–that the market doesn't offer any bargains, he's not averse to holding more than 20% of assets in cash. Plus, as much as one fourth of the fund has been invested in convertible securities–one of the largest weightings outside of the convertible-

fund group. Howard likes these hybrid securities for both their limited downside and attractive upside; they afford the capital protection of bonds, but can appreciate almost as much as the stocks' prices.

As a final safeguard, Howard frequently purchases put options on various securities; these help protect the stocks' downsides. For example, the fund owns several put options on Toys 'R' Us; both this stock and Petrie Stores, a major holder of Toys 'R' Us, have been major portfolio holdings. When Howard worried about the former firm's fortunes, he preferred to hedge the stock instead of selling it. This option proved worthwhile recently, as Toys 'R' Us stock has slid catastrophically.

Of equal importance to the fund's risk scores have been its competitive returns. True, this offering can't compete in strong bull markets, but its returns are nonetheless competitive, given its moderate volatility. The fund's big yield adds to its appeal.

History	1984	1985	1986	1987	1988	1989	1990	1991	1992	1993	1994	09-95
NAV	—	—	10.85	9.15	10.42	10.82	9.98	11.02	11.39	12.66	12.10	14.38
Total Return %	—	—	8.50 *	5.74	21.21	21.42	-1.25	21.59	9.36	15.66	3.80	18.84
+/- S&P 500	—	—	10.28 *	4.60	-0.26	-10.26	1.87	9.00	1.74	5.60	2.48	-10.89
+/- Wilshire 5000	—	—		3.38	4.60	-7.75	4.93		0.39	4.38	3.87	-11.26
Income Return %	—	—	0.00	4.88	2.90	4.25	3.7		4.51	1.49	2.85	0.00
Capital Return %	—	—	8.50	0.86	18.30	17.17	-5.0		4.85	14.17	0.95	18.84
Total Rtn %Rank All	—	—		20	11	33	59		29	26	6	33
Total Rtn %Rank Obj	—	—		23	20	67	25	87	35	18	6	94
Income $	—	—	0.00	0.48	0.28	0.45	0.39	0.43	0.50	0.18	0.35	0.00
Capital Gains $	—	—	0.00	0.85	0.37	1.36	0.31	0.64	0.16	0.33	0.69	0.00
Expense Ratio %	—	—	1.20	1.20	1.50	1.50	1.25	1.20	1.08	1.09	1.10	—
Income Ratio %	—	—	2.16	3.03	2.76	3.85	3.44	3.90	4.28	2.37	2.91	—
Turnover Rate %	—	—		291	166	99	50	51	30	39	44	—
Net Assets ($mil)	—	—	69.0	63.9	101.3	133.2	141.9	215.7	359.3	535.7	655.0	841.4

Risk Analysis

Time Period	Load-Adj Return %	Risk %Rank¹ All	Obj	Mstar Return	Morningstar Risk	Morningstar Risk-Adj Rating
1 Yr	17.42					
3 Yr	13.3			0.87	0.31	★★★★
5 Yr	15.3			0.88	0.36	★★★★
Incept	13.25			—	—	
Average Historical Rating (76 months)				4.3 ★s		

¹ 1=low, 100=high

Other Measures
	Standard Index S&P 500	Best Fit Index S&P 500
Standard Deviation	5.03	Alpha 3.3	3.3
Mean	12.71	Beta 0.53	0.53
Sharpe Ratio	1.73	R-Squared 71	71

Portfolio Analysis 06-30-95

Share Chg (12-94) 000	Amount 000	Total Stocks: 50 Total Fixed-Income: 28	Value $000	% Net Assets
	84000	Automatic Data Process Cv 0%	37170	4.76
259	959	Entergy	23141	2.96
5	180	Loews	21780	2.79
510	750	New York Times Cl A	17625	2.26
-75	365	SLMA	17110	2.19
-30	220	Philip Morris	16362	2.10
315	315	Genentech	15317	1.96
1178	2268	Petrie Stores	15308	1.96
5	53	Washington Post Cl B	13833	1.77
	550	Manville Cl B Pfd $2.70	13750	1.76
0	200	Texaco	13125	1.68
422	422	Toys 'R' Us	12340	1.58
40	260	Weyerhaeuser	12253	1.57
42	862	Manville	11854	1.52
-25	255	PHH	11348	1.45
25	275	Polaroid	11206	1.44
	11800	Rouse Cv 5.75%	10738	1.38
-5	95	Atlantic Richfield	10426	1.34
15	275	American Express	9659	1.24
130	230	Newmont Mining	9631	1.23
	10000	Delta Air Lines Cv 3.23%	9537	1.22
130	200	Kemper	9325	1.19
	8000	CIGNA Cv 8.2%	9215	1.18
	11	Cleveland Electric S Pfd $90	9202	1.18
	182	Kemper Cl E (144A) Cv Pfd	8930	1.14

Investment Style
Style Value Blend Growth	Stock Portfolio Avg	Rel S&P 500	Rel Objective
Price/Earnings Ratio	19.3	0.99	1.01
Price/Book Ratio	2.2	0.54	0.63
5 Yr Earnings Gr %	4.0	0.37	0.40
Return on Assets %	5.1	0.63	0.70
Debt % Total Cap	38.0	1.35	1.30
Med Mkt Cap ($mil)	2871	0.18	0.29

Special Securities % of assets
● Private/Illiquid Securities	6
○ Structured Notes	0
○ Emerging Markets Secs	0
○ Options/Futures/Warrants	Yes

Composition % of assets 09-30-95
Cash	22.9
Stocks	52.0
Bonds	4.0
Other	21.0

Index Allocation % of stocks
S&P 500	60.6
S&P Mid	17.0
US Sm Cap	22.5
Foreign	0.0

Sector Weightings
	% of Stocks	Rel S&P
Utilities	12.6	1.09
Energy	14.0	1.55
Financials	21.5	1.69
Industrial Cyclicals	16.4	0.98
Consumer Durables	0.0	0.00
Consumer Staples	9.2	0.37
Services	11.4	2.17
Retail	2.2	0.86
Health	8.2	0.84
Technology	0.5	0.04

Address	100 E. Pratt Street Baltimore, MD 21202	Minimum Purchase	$2500	Add: $100	IRA: $1000
Telephone	800-638-5660 / 410-54...	Min Auto Inv Plan	$50	Systematic Inv: $50	
Advisor	T. Rowe Price Associat...	* Date of Inception	06-30-86		
Subadvisor	None	**Expenses & Fees**			
Distributor	T. Rowe Price Investment Services	Sales Fees	No-load		
States Available	All plus PR	Management Fee	0.30%+0.48% max/.31% min(G)+(-).30%P		
Report Grade	A	Actual Fees	Mgt: 0.70% Dist: —		
Income Distrib	Annually	Expense Projections	3Yr: $35	5Yr: $61	10Yr: $134
		Annual Brokerage Cost	0.14%		

MORNINGSTAR Mutual Funds Ⓔ 571

THE PAGE

HIGHLIGHTS OF THE MORNINGSTAR PAGE

1. "Analysis" features written analysis of the reasons behind a fund's successes and failures.
2. "Historical Profile" shows at a glance how a fund has balanced risk and return.
3. "Portfolio Manager(s)" explains who's responsible for a fund's performance, with profiles that include work experience, education, and other funds managed.
4. Performance Quartile graph has year-by-year boxes with a dark line showing where the fund ranked.
5. "Risk Analysis" shows how a fund measures up using a variety of measures, including Morningstar risk, beta, and standard deviation.
6. "Investment Style" box helps you understand a fund's true investment strategy.
7. Investment Criteria describes the fund's investment policies and objectives.
8. "Performance" presents five years of quarterly returns. Trailing total returns for as many as seven time periods tells you if a fund leads or lags the pack.
9. "Tax Analysis" gives tax-adjusted returns and potential capital gains exposure.
10. Performance graph indicates growth of $10,000.
11. "History" lets you examine up to twelve years of statistics, including comparisons with market benchmarks, to see if the fund is a proven long-term performer.
12. "Investment Style Historical" boxes tell whether the fund follows a consistent strategy or one that changes with market conditions. You can check where it sat in the style box at the start of each calendar year.
13. "Average Stock Percentage" lets you evaluate what percentage of assets a fund has invested in stocks during each calendar year to discover if its current position is the norm or an aberration.
14. "Portfolio Analysis" reviews a fund's top stock or bond holdings to find out what's driving its performance.
15. "Sector Weightings" shows how assets are divided among ten sectors.
16. "Special Securities" explains whether a fund can and does own derivatives and other complex or illiquid securities.
17. Operations lists nuts-and-bolts information about the companies that operate and distribute the fund, including general information about fees and services.

virtually as indexes. Keep everything in context. Don't overlook the story of the manager. Many people, unfortunately, overlook it completely.

Third, located on the upper quarter of the page, the Performance Quartile Graph (Item 4 on the sample page) is composed of year-by-year boxes with a dark line showing where the fund ranked. This shows the performance quartile annually within the objective group, such as growth funds. It gives a feel for how it has done relative to other funds trying to do the same things, and also a sense of the consistency of performance. Does it lead the pack one year and trail the next, or plod along at a near-average pace for years? This data can be useful in helping people understand if a fund suits their personality.

Fourth stop in our quick tour, the "Risk Analysis" box (Item 5 on the sample page) gives a look at the fund's downside volatility relative to other similar funds. Don't overlook the risk involved with a fund. While risk relative to its broader asset class is captured up in the star rating, the risk analysis gives the risk percentile rank by objective. In Morningstar percentiles, you always want to be number one, not number 100, in performance and risk, Voss Sanders stressed, with one being the best and 100 the worst. This number allows you to see if a fund has been more or less risky than other similar funds. An equity-income fund, for example, may have a low risk score relative to other equity funds, but can be among the most volatile of the fairly tame equity-income vehicles.

Finally, use the "Investment Style" box (Item 6 on the sample page) to see if the fund uses a growth or value strategy and whether it invests in small, medium, or large companies. Because the market favors different styles at different times, it is smart to diversify a portfolio of funds across various styles.

That's the nickel tour for the time-challenged investor.

THE SCENIC ROUTE

There is, of course, more to the page than that. Take it from the top line. It first introduces you to the fund name, ticker symbol, load, NAV, yield, Securities and Exchange Commission yield, assets, and objective. Some of the major stock fund objectives include aggressive growth, equity-income, growth, growth and income, small company, foreign, and specialty funds. There are also hybrid funds that include stocks and bonds, such as asset allocation funds in which managers direct the allocating to various sectors, and balanced funds that include a set mix of stocks and bonds. On bond fund pages (the sample on page 52 is an example of a Morningstar stock fund page), the choices given include corporate bonds, municipal bonds, and adjustable-rate-mortgage securities.

Other highlights of the page include:

The Investment Criteria. This section just below the fund's name (Item 7 on sample page) describes the fund's investment policies and objectives. Information for this section comes from the description of objectives and strategies found in the fund prospectus. The first paragraph gives the fund's legal name and highlights its primary and secondary objectives, such as growth, income, or total return. The second paragraph describes the types of securities in which it invests and notes any limitations on what it may invest in. Fee structures for funds with multiple share classes may be clarified here as well. For example, Class A shares are usually sold with a front-end sales charge, while Class B shares may be sold with a declining deferred sales charge and a higher annual 12B-1 fee to cover distribution and marketing costs.

Performance. Here Morningstar calculates total returns by taking the change in NAV (Item 8 on sample page), assuming the reinvestment of all income and capital gains distributions, and divides it by the initial NAV. It does not adjust the total returns in this section for sales charges or redemption fees. The fund's short- and long-term total returns are compared to other funds and various indexes. The fund's benchmark index is the one most representative of the fund's objective class, giving the investor a point of reference for evaluating performance. One column shows the current value of a $10,000 investment made at the beginning of each of the time periods listed.

Most Similar Funds in MMF. This item located within the Performance section identifies the three funds that have the most similar performance characteristics based on historical total returns. It does not measure the similarity of portfolio holdings. To determine the similarity of a fund, Morningstar calculates a linear regression line for each fund against every other fund. It's helpful if an investor wants to buy shares in a fund that has closed to new investors and must choose a substitute instead.

Tax Analysis. Use this section (Item 9 on sample page) to evaluate a fund's after-tax returns, its efficiency in achieving them, and the amount of capital gains. The first statistic is the tax-adjusted historical return, showing the fund's annualized after-tax total return for the three-, five-, and ten-year periods. In addition, the percentage pretax return statistic measures the tax efficiency by dividing after-tax returns by pretax returns. The potential capital gains exposure figure, based on a fund's unrealized appreciation, can provide a glimpse of a shareholder's vulnerability to future taxation. However, taxes, like risk, should be considered in the context of all other aspects of a fund. There will be more on tax implications later in this book.

Performance Graph. This shows how $10,000 has grown in the fund (Item 10 on sample page). Along its vertical axis are the dollar amounts shown in thousands, while along the bottom of the graph are the preceding twelve calendar years. In addition to showing fund performance, the graph shows performance of $10,000 in a relevant bench-mark index, either the S&P 500 Index or the Lehman Brothers Aggregate Bond Index.

History. This table (Item 11 on sample page) lets you examine up to twelve years of statistics, including compar-ison with market benchmarks, to see if the fund is a proven long-term performer. The table below the graph includes annual returns, distributions, and expenses. The annual expense ratio expresses the percentage of assets deducted each fiscal year for fund operating expenses, including the 12b-1 fees, management fees, administrative fees, operating costs, and all other asset-based costs incurred by the fund, except for brokerage costs. In addition, the small "Investment Style Historical" boxes (Item 12 on sample page) near the top of the page tell whether the fund fol-lows a consistent strategy or one that changes with market conditions, while the "Average Stock Percentage" figures (Item 13 on sample page) lets you evaluate what percent-age of assets a fund has invested in stocks during each cal-endar year.

Risk Analysis. In addition to showing the Morningstar risk and return statistics that make up the star rating, a fund's load-adjusted returns are listed for the trailing three, five-, and ten-year periods. You'll recall that risk analysis (Item 5 on sample page) was a stop on the nickel tour.

Other Measures. These items located just below the Risk Analysis section are derived from modern portfolio theory. For example, *alpha* measures the difference between a fund's actual returns and its expected performance, given its level of risk. A positive alpha figure indicates the fund has performed better than its beta would predict. *Beta* is a measure of a fund's sensitivity to market movements. The beta of the benchmark index is 1.00, so a fund with a 1.10 beta is expected to perform 10 percent better. Another term, *R-squared*, reflects the percentage of a fund's move-ments that are explained by movements in its benchmark index. An R-squared of 100 means that all movements of a fund are completely explained by movements in the index. A low R-squared indicates few of the fund's movements are explained by movements in its benchmark index. Another useful measure is the standard deviation, a statistical gauge of the range of performance within which a fund's total returns have fallen. The *standard deviation* figure provided by Morningstar is an annualized statistic based on thirty-six monthly returns.

Portfolio Analysis. The fund's most recently reported top holdings—usually twenty-five of them—and information such as the size of the portfolio's investment in a specific security are displayed here (Item 14 on sample page). This gives the investor the ability to identify exactly what drives a fund's performance. With stock funds, the share change entry indicates the change in number of shares of each stock from the previously reported portfolio. This gives clues as to management strategy. The amount column refers to the size of the portfolio's investment in a given security. For fixed-income holdings, maturity of the individual bond is listed to the right of the security.

Investment Style. This section in the lower right-hand portion of the page presents a statistical analysis of a fund's investment nature, using a combination of measures such as price/earnings (P/E) ratio and price/book (P/B) ratio. The P/E of a stock is calculated by dividing the current price by its trailing twelve months' earnings per share. The first statistic in this section is the weighted average of the P/E ratios of stocks in the portfolio. A high P/E indicates that the market is paying more to obtain the stock because of confidence in its ability to increase its earnings. A low P/E means the market has less confidence that earnings will rise, and therefore isn't willing to pay as much. A fund with a high average P/E ratio has paid a premium for stocks with high potential, while a fund with low average P/E may hold stocks its manager believes are undervalued. The price/book ratio of a company is calculated by dividing the market price of its stock by the company's per-share book value.

The P/B ratio listed by Morningstar is the weighted average of the ratios of all the stocks in the portfolio. In theory, a high P/B ratio indicates the price of the stock exceeds the actual worth of the company's assets, while a low ratio indicates the stock is a bargain. Five-year earnings growth included here is a measure of the trailing five-year annualized earnings growth record of stocks in the portfolio. Median market capitalization of companies in an equity portfolio is listed, while in bond funds the average effective maturity provided is a weighted average of all the maturities in the portfolio.

Investment Style Box. Located within the Investment Style section and discussed in the nickel tour, this popular equity style box (Item 6 on sample page) is a nine-box matrix that displays a summary of a portfolio's characteristics and permits the reader to determine a fund's investment objectives. For stock funds, the style box displays both the fund's investment methodology and the size of companies in which it invests. Combining these two variables offers a broad view of a fund's holdings and risk. Morningstar categorizes a fund's style as growth-oriented, value-oriented, or a blend of the two, while the market capitalization is rated as small, medium, or large. Meanwhile, the fixed-income "Investment Style" box, included only on the Morningstar bond fund page, focuses instead on interest rate sensitivity and credit quality.

Composition, Sector Weightings, and Special Securities. These three sections in the lowest right-hand corner of the page constitute part of the portfolio analysis. The "Composition" percentages provide a simple breakdown of the fund's portfolio holdings into general investment classes. In the case of foreign funds, the top five countries in which a fund is invested are also listed. The "Sector

Weightings" (Item 15 on sample page) show the percentage of the fund's equity assets invested in each of ten major industry classifications, revealing the areas that a fund favors and those it avoids. Major industries include utilities, energy, financial, industrial cyclicals, consumer durables, consumer staples, services, retail, health, and technology. On bond pages (once again, not shown on the sample page), there is bond fund information on bond types, credit quality, and the coupons, or rates of interest.

The "Special Securities" section (Item 16 on sample page) shows a fund's exposure to a variety of complex or illiquid securities, including derivatives. Information is compiled from the portfolio listed in a fund's most recent shareholder report.

Operations. Located at the bottom left-hand side of the page (Item 17 on sample page), this section lists nuts-and-bolts information about the companies that operate and distribute the fund, including general information about fees and services. For example, there's an address and telephone number to request a prospectus. The advisor listed is the company that takes primary responsibility for managing the fund, though in some cases the company hires a subadvisor to handle daily management. In the sales fees included here, no-load indicates that a fund charges no sales or 12b-1 fees. If there's a front-end sales or deferred sales charge, it is included here. The maximum 12b-1 fee represents the maximum annual charge deducted from fund assets to pay for distribution and marketing. The management fee is the percentage deducted from a fund's average net assets to pay an advisor or subadvisor, while the maximum administrative fee is the maximum allowable charge for administrative costs, excluding advisor fees. Morningstar also evaluates the quality of the report of funds sent to shareholders, on a scale from A+ to F.

That, in a nutshell, is the page. It's an amazingly compact

Morningstar Portfolio Developer – Client 1			
File	Edit	View	Option	Help

| 🕐 📷 Snapshot | Update | Sector Weightings |

12 Portfolio Holdings	Allocation %
Allocation Total	100.0
Gabelli Asset	2.13
Linder Dividend	4.25
Montgomery Emerging Markets	2.13
Selected American	2.13
T. Row Price New Icome	5.32
T. Row Price New Era	5.32
Fidelity Disciplined Equity	5.32
Fidelity Low-Priced Stock	5.32
Brandywine	53.19
Vanguard International Growth	6.38
PBHG Growth	2.13
Vanguard Index 500	6.38

	Portfolio	S&P 500
Utilities	11.85	11.60
Energy	8.53	9.09
Financial	8.28	12.78
Industrial Cyclicals	11.73	16.68
Consumer Durables	7.71	4.50
Consumer Staples	2.12	11.37
Services	6.15	8.22
Retail	5.39	4.89
Health	5.55	9.85
Technology	32.69	11.01

0 10 20 30 40 50 60 70 80 90 100

Wave of the Future

Electronic products, designed to help investors and professionals compare investments more easily than with the traditional printed product, increase the ability to track one's personal portfolio. This example breaks down the allocation of an individual's holdings and indicates sector weightings.

bundle of information with which the company still tinkers on a regular basis to deliver the most pertinent items.

Morningstar's ongoing expansion into electronic products does more than simply transfer the page to the computer screen. Besides delivering the factual information and familiar features of the MMF binder, these new products are designed to permit greater flexibility in screening for investment criteria and directly comparing fund choices. By entering the proper commands rather than flipping through pages, one need look only at the information that he or she deems pertinent (see example of electronic product on page 61). The goal is to employ the speed and depth of computer software to formulate and track a personalized portfolio.

Whatever the vehicle, MMF analysts have an ambitious task in helping to pull everything together week after week. As young as most Morningstar analysts are, neither the industry nor investors ever permit them to lapse into shortsightedness. One veteran portfolio manager once sternly admonished his Morningstar questioner: "Well, young lady, fifteen years may seem long-term to you, but at my age it's not!"

CHAPTER 5

∎

5-STAR WARS

"The 5-star rating is a double-edged sword. It's a valid way of evaluating funds on a risk-adjusted methodology to find those that have achieved the best returns for a given level of risk. It ferrets out all-weather funds that have done consistently well. But it gets abused when people think of it as the be-all and end-all. Consider it a nice entry point to a whole host of items to look at, but definitely not the end point."
—JOE MANSUETO, MORNINGSTAR
FOUNDER AND CHAIRMAN

We're a 5-star fund."

For many investors, the 5-star rating system is Morningstar's best-known attribute because fund companies are always bragging about it. It's splattered all over advertisements by mutual fund companies. One of the proudest statements that a portfolio manager ever makes is that his fund is, indeed, among those bearing the coveted Morningstar 5-star rating.

But, as with most rating systems, it's also been the most controversial aspect of Morningstar's work. It reminds me a bit of a complaint I've heard lodged a number of times by the film critic tandem of Gene Siskel and Roger Ebert. When both of them like a particular movie, the subtle nuances of their individual reviews are often wiped out altogether in film advertisements. All that appears are the words: "Two thumbs up: Siskel & Ebert." Each understandably believes he has much more guidance to offer the potential moviegoer than that oversimplified and likely misleading message.

Morningstar subscribers have come to understand the star ratings much better in the 1990s due to the company's ongoing and careful depiction of them as a risk/reward measure that summarizes a fund's history. However, some financial professionals and investors who laud Morningstar for the overall accuracy and volume of its data disagree with the use of its star ratings. The system has also been an ongoing target of some fund managers, competitors, and industry observers, with several organizations producing numbers that they believe denigrate the 5-star's market-timing ability.

Misunderstandings can also extend to individual investors. I still recall one senior citizen pulling me aside one day to whisper in an incredulous tone that "I bought a 5-star fund, and it went down." It was as if the star rating was a shield against all the potential for volatility in the world's financial markets. Part of this is Morningstar's own fault. In its early years, the company borrowed Wall Street terminology and labeled 5-star funds "buy" and 1-star funds "sell," a practice that was dropped in 1990. The rating's real purpose, however, has always been to sort funds according to past success and provide a starting point for further evaluation.

What exactly is a star rating, anyway? Well, it pulls both risk and performance together into one evaluation and, to Morningstar's way of thinking, is a historical rather than a predictive tool.

Morningstar believes that most investors' greatest fear is losing money. It defines that as underperforming the risk-free rate of return an investor can earn from the 90-day Treasury bill. To calculate the risk score, Morningstar plots monthly fund returns in relation to T-bill returns. It adds up the amounts by which the fund trails the T-bill return each month and divides that total by the period's total number of months. This number, the average monthly underperformance statistic, is then compared with those of other funds in the same broad investment category to assign risk scores. The resulting score expresses how risky the fund is relative to the average fund in its category. The average risk score for the category is set equal to 1.00. For example, a Morningstar risk score of 1.35 for a taxable bond fund means that the fund has been 35 percent riskier than the average taxable bond fund for the period considered.

The other major component in the star rating, the Morningstar return figure, rates a fund's performance relative to other funds in its investment category. After adjusting for maximum front-end loads, applicable deferred loads, and applicable redemption fees, Morningstar calculates the excess return for each fund. It is defined as the fund's load-adjusted return minus the return for 90-day T-bills over the same period. The use of excess instead of raw returns reflects Morningstar's belief that mutual funds should be rated highly for only those returns earned beyond those of a T-bill. The excess returns are then compared with the higher of the average excess return of the fund's broad investment class or the 90-day T-bill return. The resulting Morningstar return figure is listed relative to the average excess return of the investment category or the T-bill, whichever is higher.

To determine a particular fund's star rating for a given period, the fund's risk score is subtracted from its return score. The resulting number is plotted along a bell curve to determine the fund's rating for each time period. If the fund scores in the top 10 percent of its broad investment category it receives 5 stars (highest). If it falls in the next 22.5 percent, it receives 4 stars (above average). A place in the middle 35 percent earns it 3 stars (below average) and those in the next 22.5 percent receive 2 stars (below average). The bottom 10 percent get 1 star (lowest). The star ratings are recalculated monthly.

In answer to a questionnarie I sent to portfolio managers and financial planners, most said they thought the 5-star ratings were helpful, but that they can indeed be misconstrued by the uninitiated. Most applauded the goal of getting a handle on risk and performance in one measure. Separate interviews I conducted with fund managers backed that belief up as well. "We don't use the 5-star ratings in our advertising, but brokers do use it," said Shelby Davis, portfolio manager of the Davis New York Venture and Selected American Shares funds. "Risk is an important consideration because the stock market tends to give higher price/earnings to those with steady results rather than cyclical movement, and the same thing would seem to be true of mutual funds."

Those who receive better ratings are generally the most positive about the system. "I feel the idea of defining risk is a squishy notion and I see nothing inherently wrong with trying to do it," said Gary Pilgrim, portfolio manager of PBHG Growth Fund. "We're volatile, but we've been able to make up for it with our returns. We're 5-star and we see nothing out of balance with the Morningstar ratings." There's also a belief that while it's impossible to come up with a 100 percent acceptable measure of risk because it's a difficult concept to pin down, it does merit attention. "It seems very likely that risk characteristics are predictable and identifiable, and knowing risk is certainly quite useful," observed Ralph Wanger, manager of the Acorn Fund.

But the rankings provoke disagreement. "Morningstar is a useful service that's the best in the mutual fund area, but its star system is flawed because 90 percent of people believe 5-star rankings are predictive," contends Jerome Dodson, portfolio manager of the 3-star-rated Parnassus Fund, who believes his fund's strong performance deserves far more consideration than its volatility. "The problem is that it gives a premium to the fact that not having fluctuations means you'll get a high rating, even if you have a lower return as well." Former Vanguard Group chairman Jack Bogle, in his book *Bogle on Mutual Funds*, called Morningstar a "peerless" source of information on funds, but said its star system "appears to have little predictive value." A better indicator, to his way of thinking, is Morningstar's highlighting of each fund's annual total return relative to the other funds in its objective category.

Morningstar acknowledges its system favors certain types of funds at the expense of others. Among the biggest beneficiaries are short-term bond funds. Because shorter bond funds tend to garner most of longer funds' returns at a fraction of their volatility, they usually dominate risk-adjusted measurements. As a result, shorter-term bond funds crowded the fixed-income 5-star list a decade ago and they still do today. The 5-star bond funds generally trail their peers during flat to bull markets, as in 1991–93, and lead during bear markets, as in 1994. Because bull markets have predominated over the past decade, 5-star bond funds have posted lower aggregate returns than their peers. They will likely do so over the next decade as well unless interest rates rise. These funds' volatility is generally low, which suggests that their asset-weighted gains may match their flashier rivals.

"While I think Morningstar is one of the best things out there, I see an overemphasis in its star ratings on the volatility of bonds, rather than on their quality," asserted Reid Smith, manager of a number of Vanguard Group municipal bond portfolios. "The higher-quality bond funds are more priced to the market, more liquid, and more volatile, so lower-grade bonds receive a better Morningstar rating because they don't trade frequently and are less volatile." Smith believes his funds get "beaten up" on volatility because he runs insured funds, which are the most liquid of all and always bounce around in price. As a result, they generally receive only 3- and 4-star ratings despite good returns. Lower-grade bond funds of competitors won't show volatility until they blow up altogether someday, Smith warns. Furthermore, the call risk of many of these funds isn't addressed by the ratings. In summation, Smith believes good ratings shouldn't be given to junk bonds or funds with callability just because they don't move much.

Knowing what will happen with top-rated stock funds is an even trickier proposition. Unlike the ratings for bond funds, the star ratings for stock funds do not fit a consistent pattern. They depend upon prevailing market conditions over the past several years. Trends that can greatly affect star ratings include a string of good years from industry groups, such as financials and technology during the 1990s; domestic versus international results; and whether large or small companies have been doing better. Because these trends sometimes persist after they have pushed funds to top ratings and other times suddenly reverse course, 5-star stock funds show highly variable short-term relative performance. For example, stock funds carrying 5-star ratings at the beginning of recent calendar years fared poorly in 1993, about average in 1994, and extraordinarily well in 1995.

"I think the star ratings are distracting for some people," remarked John Markese, president of the American Association of Individual Investors, who otherwise is an admirer of Morningstar's publications. "For example, Morningstar may list some groups, such as international funds, with only one or two stars because ratings are weighted to recent performance. As a result, people won't buy an international fund."

Investors should realize that it's okay to buy a fund with a lower star rating if it represents a group they consider likely to do well in the future. The ratings of international stock funds probably provide the clearest indication of the power of market trends. When *Morningstar Mutual Funds* first came out in 1986, most international stock funds had 4- and 5-star ratings due to thriving overseas markets. They continued to prosper during the publication's first two years, then began to falter as the domestic markets returned to the forefront. Most recently, the typical foreign or world stock fund carries just 2 or 3 stars. Even within the international stock grouping, other effects have triggered gyrations in fund ratings, such as their exposure to emerging markets. Funds with many emerging-market assets looked great in the early 1990s, but suddenly slid into a protracted ratings slide.

Style effects don't disappear when domestic stock funds are considered either. Early in Morningstar's history, during the mid-1980s, large, inexpensive companies were the biggest domestic-stock gainers, while aggressive, higher-risk stocks lagged. Since 1989, the pattern has been the opposite. Morningstar's most recent ratings therefore favor higher-risk funds. Funds in the growth and bolder specialty fund categories, such as technology, communications, and financials, have had twice the representation of 5-star funds than one would expect, while more conservative blend and hybrid funds were sharply underrepresented.

Even though Morningstar itself argues against it, various studies of the 5-star rankings inevitably consider whether they're predictive of future success. Critics contend that no matter what Morningstar may say investors always buy something that's 5-star because they believe it's the best and will do well for them in the future.

"Morningstar's analysis of funds and statistics is impressive and it deserves kudos, but it's struggling with the fact that the past is not a true indicator of the future," argues Mark Hulbert, editor of *The Hulbert Financial Digest*, which tracks the nation's investment letters. "The 5-star ranking system has changed over the years, and now Morningstar says it is simply historical about how funds have done on a risk-adjusted basis, and is not prospective." Using the Morningstar star ratings, Hulbert invests a hypothetical $10,000 into designated funds, as he does with all of the nation's investment letters. In the case of load funds, he charges the load and gets out of a fund as soon as it's no longer on the 5-star list. According to Hulbert's computations, over a five-year period both the load and no-load group of 5-star funds failed to beat the Wilshire 5000.

Morningstar argues that this is a misuse of its ratings, since the 5-star funds are not presented as a model portfolio. It also disagrees with Hulbert's charging of loads or redemption fees each time a load fund makes it on the 5-star list and another exits. It contends that it isn't recommending the sale of a fund and its replacement each and every time a change occurs in the ratings. That contention is not, however, accepted by Hulbert, who believes the 5-stars should be considered a portfolio and tracked as such.

In addition, archcompetitor Lipper Analytical Services conducted its own study of Morningstar 5-star performance. In 1994, it took Morningstar 5-star funds in the beginning of 1990, 1991, 1992, and 1993 and then looked at how the funds performed in the next twelve months. The company said its results showed that a majority of 5-star stock funds did worse in the rest of the year than the average stock fund, while the majority of 5-star taxable bond funds did worse than the average bond fund in three of the four years. "In our view, the real problem involves salespeople who use the Morningstar 5-star rating as some kind of judgment on a fund," said A. Michael Lipper, president of Lipper Analytical Services. "It has nothing to do with risk, because volatility versus T-bills isn't risk."

Morningstar itself has done some research on the performance of 5-star funds and, as always, its primary concern was with longer-term results rather than with one-year movements.

With rare exception, those stock funds posting 5-star ratings at *Morningstar Mutual Fund's* 1986 debut notched respectable or better results during the next nine years, a study conducted by Morningstar's John Rekenthaler found. Some, such as Fidelity Magellan and Mutual Shares, were downright brilliant. The 5-star funds of 1986 became market leaders that now command headlines, praise, and billion-dollar asset bases. Conversely, more than a dozen 1-star stock funds have performed so badly as to be merged out of existence, or to have no real hope of attracting future assets. Few have rebounded sufficiently to achieve industry prominence. So, in the one shot the star ratings have had at indicating stock funds' true long-term prospects, they've done a great job.

From the 5-star diversified stock funds of 1986, the winners have been Fidelity Equity-Income, Fidelity Magellan, the Lindner Fund, Mutual Qualified Income, Mutual Shares, Neuberger & Berman Partners, Selected American Shares, Sequoia Fund, SoGen International, and Vanguard Windsor. There were no losers.

Meanwhile, from the 1-star funds of that same year, winners have been AIM Constellation, Berger 100, Kaufmann Fund, Keystone S-4, and Twentieth Century Ultra. Losers have been American Investors Growth, Fairfield, First Investors Discovery, 44 Wall Street, 44 Wall Street Equity,

Fund of the Southwest, Leverage Fund of Boston, Lowry Market Timing, Nautilus, Rochester Growth, Sherman Dean, Sierra Growth, Steadman American Industries, Steadman Oceanographic, Strategic Capital Gains, United Services Growth, Value Line Special Situations, and Westergaard Fund.

Outside forces can place greater emphasis on the star rating system than Morningstar itself does. For example, Morningstar reluctantly added a one-year star rating, a measure it believes places an unhealthy emphasis on short-term performance, to its Principia mutual fund software in May 1996. No subscribers had requested such an addition and Morningstar was dead-set against it, but the National Association of Securities Dealers had demanded its inclusion. NASD top brass contended that showing data for not just longer-term three-, five-, and ten-year periods, but also the latest year, "really rounds out the picture" when comparing similar funds. This pressure exerted in long-running negotiations between the NASD and the firm was understandably effective. Without the disputed change, the agency could have possibly stopped NASD-regulated brokers and investment advisors from distributing Morningstar research to their clients. Morningstar still harbors hopes that the one-year star rating at some point can be discontinued.

The first question that many people ask about the star rating is not "Will it put me in good long-term funds?" but rather "How has it worked as a market-timing device?" That's because all investments tend to be discussed in terms of short-term results, not as a long-term, risk-adjusted measure. In attempting to change that tradition, the star ratings must break a lot of accumulated habits on the part of both financial professionals and average investors.

Morningstar has been doing all it can to change the image, injecting caveats every time it mentions the 5-star rating and even changing the name of the *5-Star Investor* to the *Morningstar Investor*. It does see a change occurring in how the rating is perceived, for the questions it receives from subscribers indicate that most of them use the star ratings in the intended role of a first-stage investment screen. Responses to the questionnaires I sent to financial planners and portfolio managers exhibited the same comprehension of what the stars were really all about. These folks clearly do not swap 5-star funds in the manner that some experts assume they do. Instead, they view the 5-star rating as offering a quick idea about which funds have been successful and which have not. The presumption is that the successful group constitutes a better starting point. Morningstar believes that is the true context in which the stars should ultimately be judged.

CHAPTER 6

■

FUND FAMILY VALUES

"You could cost yourself a lot of money by sticking exclusively with a weaker fund family. Individuals with a substantial amount of money in a lower-rated company should reexamine their holdings now."
—JOHN REKENTHALER, MORNINGSTAR
PUBLISHER OF MANAGED PRODUCTS

Call it the "fund with no name" experience. It's a lot like a wine tasting in which all of the labeled bottles are kept out of sight in the back room so no one knows exactly which vintner produced what's being sipped.

At a regular meeting of Morningstar analysts, one of the editors passes out copies of a typical *Morningstar Mutual Fund* page that spotlights a specific fund. Only difference is that the name of the fund, its fund family, and the portfolio manager's name have all been blacked out. So have the written analysis and the name of the analyst who penned it.

The basic question of this exercise is: What story would you tell about this fund based on the page's data? Discussion ensues, with analysts noting the history, volatility, returns, and potential of the nameless fund. Inevitably, everyone tries to guess which fund it really is. That's where the fun begins. Often a fund may be from a family for which there are lower expectations, or whose reputation is for an entirely different strategy than the fund in question depicts. This gets the staff to concentrate on pure analysis rather than on how popular the fund family is, how friendly the fund manager is, or how helpful its public relations staff may be.

Surprisingly, then, some wine without a label tastes better than expected. In other cases, a famous family offering may not live up to its name.

Many investors, unfortunately, never take such a dispassionate, critical view when selecting mutual funds.

Each day they see image-conscious television commercials that show grainy film clips of a hard-nosed, bespectacled Dean Witter character before a fireplace urging his brokers to press onward in serving clients with all their souls. They watch the mighty Dreyfus lion roar boldly on Wall Street, throwing a scare into a rampaging bull that quickly changes direction. It's heady stuff.

But investors probably don't realize that Dean Witter and Dreyfus have been perhaps the worst-performing and least-focused of the major mutual fund families, marching a legion of trusting investors into lackluster returns.

On the other hand, some investors may believe that Fidelity's high profile is primarily due to the long-term success of its giant Magellan Fund and the firm's considerable marketing muscle, and therefore dismiss its other offerings as also-rans. That's another big mistake because, while

Fidelity isn't tops in every single category, its overall performance ranks first among fund families.

The uninitiated are swayed by the sound of the fund family's name, its perceived reputation, or the pressure of a high-powered salesperson, not the actual investment facts at hand. Worse yet, they may think that all fund families offer pretty much the same products with similar performance.

Fund families, which group together a number of funds under one corporate banner, are a crucial consideration because many investors still buy from one company for the sake of convenience. In addition, various self-directed and company retirement accounts are often captive to one designated family. It's possible to discover a fine-performing fund within a group whose overall results are lackluster, though it's usually best to avoid families that are truly dysfunctional.

Morningstar has the inside track in understanding and comparing the largest mutual fund families. Its contact with these companies from top to bottom, as well as its analysis of their returns and strategies, can provide an incisive view.

This is Morningstar's evaluation of the nation's largest mutual fund families:

FIDELITY

It's big for some excellent reasons. Fidelity Management and Research stands out as the leader in the mutual fund industry in terms of not only total assets, but marketing, image, and domestic stock investment results as well. It hasn't done quite as well with international stock funds or with fixed-income funds, but it's still competitive in those areas. Fidelity is an innovator in the technological aspects of running a fund business, as well as in the motivation and training of portfolio managers. Like Morningstar, Fidelity gives a high degree of responsibility to young managers. It has a range of funds including no-load, low-load, and full-load.

If Fidelity had been a publicly traded stock and Morningstar staffers were permitted to buy stocks of fund companies, several said they'd have bought it, made a lot of money with it, and would still be holding it. Of course, the fact the company is not publicly traded is a major reason why it's been able to plow so much money back into technological advances and other crucial aspects of its business. It should continue to hold its preeminent position in the fund industry with its low-load funds unless it somehow gets caught on the wrong side of a bear market or makes some enormous overall mistake in its corporate philosophy.

Fidelity chairman Edward C. "Ned" Johnson III was once a portfolio manager himself and has worked hard to create an environment that is ideal for a manager, devoid of the all too common marketing pressure to be out on the road giving speeches all the time. As a result, it's possible for the staff to focus on money management while enjoying the finest resources available. In fact, there's a real question as to why any manager would ever leave Fidelity of his own will, since it offers the best research, best access to Wall Street, and some of the best pay in the industry. Too often Fidelity is viewed as a marketing machine, while the unique investment climate is overlooked.

This company faces great public and government scrutiny due to its size, and is willing to make tough decisions. For example, in the most sweeping management realignment in its history, Fidelity reassigned twenty-six of its equity portfolio managers in April 1996. That represented almost one-third of its stock funds. Improving performance, putting funds more in line with stated objectives, and assuring that high risks are avoided were behind that move. Earlier in the year, the company had also begun monitoring more closely which issues its fund managers buy, withdrew from activist investment in distressed securities, got out of risky bond investments, and determined which of its funds would be permitted to invest in volatile emerging markets. That's definitely not a company resting on its laurels.

VANGUARD

Number two tries just as hard. As the second-largest mutual fund company, Vanguard Group demonstrates there is no one path to success in money management. This outstanding no-load organization is the antithesis of Fidelity. Its strength is its low cost structure, producing a set of funds designed to benefit from that positive factor. No-load Vanguard is a not-for-profit company owned collectively by the shareholders of its funds, giving it a significant cost advantage over everyone else in the industry. Its index products and straightforward fixed-income products are highly successful as a result. Vanguard is an inherently conservative group because those lower costs mean it doesn't have to take the same risks as other groups in order to get the same returns.

Founder and former chairman Jack Bogle, a shrewd competitor who retired from active management in early 1996, was the one individual who really got under Fidelity's skin. He was much better at pure public relations than Fidelity and in many ways served as the corporate symbol of Vanguard. His stamp has been on every product and marketing strategy. Still, nobody can match Fidelity's record for actively managed domestic stock funds. Vanguard hasn't been distinguished in that area, running moderately above average in stock fund performance, since its cost advantage is less important there. Its stock fund offerings include a couple of fine products and not too many dreadful ones.

Despite its conservative nature, Vanguard has the ability

79

to surprise. In early 1996, this penny-pinching firm further reduced the annual advisory fees on seventeen of its stock and bond funds representing a total of $56 billion in assets and including some of its most popular actively managed funds. Advisory fees represent a portion of the annual expense of owning a mutual fund. Even though it's recognized as the lowest-cost producer, Vanguard's strategy obviously hasn't shifted to automatic pilot.

MERRILL LYNCH

The Merrill Lynch bull has been forcing other brokerage house fund competitors to consistently eat its dust. Even competitors would grudgingly concede that it's the best, and in private conversations executives of those other brokerage houses often say they'd like to be more like the Merrill Lynch Group. It has been, for example, smart enough to keep the hands of its marketing staff out of its new product development. Ultimately, every fund company defines itself by the kinds of products it launches and how well it presents them to the public. Merrill Lynch didn't come up with the more gimmicky funds other brokerage firms offered and that's a good thing, since they eventually blew up in investors' faces.

It didn't offer any option income funds or government plus funds (government bond funds that used options trading to try to inflate their yields). Its high-yield fund wasn't among those that took a bath, unlike those of some competitors. The only real miscue of this load group was offering a short-term multi-market fund, but it came out publicly later to acknowledge that it had indeed made a mistake. That's an unusual step in the stiff-upper-lip investment world. It made that admission at the very same time that many other companies were scrambling to defend their plummeting short-term multi-market vehicles.

Merrill Lynch has featured a strong value orientation in its stock mutual funds. It also got into international stock funds ahead of the competition in the 1980s and has built a strong position in this legitimate long-term growth segment. The weakness of the company, however, is that while it has come up with some good, serviceable, dependable products and run them cleanly, it hasn't really been all that excellent at anything in particular. Despite good performances from some of its funds, it hasn't displayed tremendous skill in portfolio management.

AMERICAN FUNDS

It turns its competitors green with envy. A quality family of funds, American Funds Group is considered *the* first family of load funds. Discussions with executives of other load fund families time and time again will bring up the wish that their operations could become more like American. While Fidelity has brash young managers who are given high visibility for the work they do, American uses a "multiple portfolio counselor" system that means low visibility and no star managers. The people running its funds tend to spend decades on the job with little turnover. Its investment committees are a bit different than usual, in that the company actually has portions of its portfolios run by different people. A manager typically has complete autonomy over his specific section.

American's strengths have been its huge growth and its income funds, as well as international investing. Its weak point, however, is its fixed-income products, where it hasn't excelled. In most of its strong areas, it comes up with a relatively limited group of well-defined products that it's proud of and it sticks with them. American Funds is popular with financial planners. While there are a lot of ways to turn a load fund into a no-load fund these days, American hasn't gone that route because its dominance in its field means such tinkering just isn't necessary. Moreover, American professes a strong belief in the value of a financial planner. It has not, for example, come up with separate no-load B shares as many other load families have done.

FRANKLIN TEMPLETON

Ben Franklin would've been proud of this publicly traded company. Run by an intelligent staff, Franklin Templeton is the fund group that resulted from the merger of the Franklin and Templeton groups. Franklin was a huge success in the 1980s in fixed-income investing, raking in an enormous amount of money as it built a powerful franchise from an extremely small base. Franklin's fund loads are mostly in the mid range of around 4 percent, while Templeton's are 5.75 percent. Because the majority of its assets were in fixed-rate choices highly vulnerable to increases in domestic interest rates, it intelligently made a move to purchase the much-admired Templeton Group. This immediately gave it strength in the international arena with the dynamic group of funds that Sir John Templeton pioneered.

Financial planners have often overlooked Franklin Templeton's domestic stock funds, but that is changing. In mid-1996, the firm agreed to purchase Michael Price's Heine Securities Inc., which manages the popular Mutual Series stock funds. While it paid a hefty price tag of more than $500 million, Franklin Templeton received a premier name that should benefit from expanded marketing efforts. It makes Franklin Templeton a powerhouse in fixed-income, international stocks, and domestic stocks.

DREYFUS

This famous lion, which offers mostly no-load funds, should whimper rather than roar. Dreyfus Group, a widely known and highly visible family of funds that was a 1970s pioneer with the money market mutual fund, is an enigma in the fund industry. It really hasn't capitalized on its early success and unfortunately launched a number of rather odd funds with the word "strategy" in their name in the 1980s. These wide-open funds permitted their managers to do a lot of different things, but having much investment success wasn't one of them.

Dreyfus has a worrisome tendency to err on the side of extreme conservatism. When most fund companies try something different, the process usually involves taking on a greater degree of risk. At Dreyfus, a fund labeled a stock fund might somehow wind up a parking place for a huge amount of assets in cash. There has never, for example, ever been a junk bond fund at Dreyfus. This overall conservatism certainly hasn't helped this fund group during an extended bull market. Its funds have been in an extended slump. Despite having at least one excellent stock fund manager, Tom Frank, Dreyfus stock funds as a whole are quite mediocre, especially when the comparison is made to a powerhouse such as Fidelity. It also has a relatively small investment management staff and isn't known for overspending on portfolio managers.

You can't point to Dreyfus and say it has any one great strength. Another problem is that right now the company is neither fish nor fowl, in that it was acquired by Mellon Bank but didn't really have a strong group of load funds to distribute through that channel. Most of its offerings have been low-load or no-load funds. Dreyfus still has a great name in the industry and its lion is a powerful corporate symbol, but it unfortunately lost some good managers following the acquisition by Mellon. It simply doesn't have a viable game plan. There's also been a history of bad timing in the introduction of new funds, such as its electric utilities fund introduced at the market peak for that group. You can guess what happened next.

PUTNAM

This group has been born again. After stumbling badly in the late 1980s with option-oriented funds that scarred the firm and tarnished its name in the brokerage and financial planning communities, Putnam Mutual Funds is on the rise. The prior culprits had been two option income funds and a government plus fund, all of them winding up as utter disasters. The group has since rebounded and is now patterning itself after American Funds. It realizes that that sort of status isn't achieved overnight, but only comes as a result of delivering consistently good performance.

This well-managed load fund firm isn't truly exceptional at any one type of fund. But it is above average in a number of areas, such as international, domestic stock, and fixed-income. That makes its product line an exceptional choice for sale by banks, financial planners, brokerage firms, and large pension funds. It is also a solid competitor for the 401(k) retirement account market.

DEAN WITTER

Shame, shame. Though improving, Dean Witter Funds has represented the worst-case scenario among brokerage house fund groups. It has plenty of assets thanks to its enormous and energetic sales staff that pushes its in-house products hard, but doesn't have much success to go along with it. It consistently hurt investors with overpromised, bad, and ill-conceived products. While Merrill Lynch has come out with clean, straightforward products that don't get too tricky, Dean Witter has always chosen aggressively run funds with very little hedging of bets. It always tries to push the accelerator to the floor, and relies on its sales force to convince clients that its ideas will work effectively.

This load fund group often introduced novice investors to aggressively run funds in sectors that had peaked, as it did with a growth stock fund after a three-year growth stock run. Similarly, a health care fund, a junk bond fund, and a convertible securities fund were also introduced at the least advantageous times. When a bear market in a poorly chosen sector occurs, the fund gets particularly hurt because it's so aggressive. Of course, a great many investors never made any money on the upside of these groups because they got in at the top.

While Dean Witter has strong brand name recognition, it hasn't had a product lineup that sophisticated fund investors have found attractive. It also has done a terrible job of communicating what its funds do, and its relationship with the press has often been hostile. It has often gone after less sophisticated investors who weren't so aware of its poor brand reputation, such as those that invest through its kiosks located in Sears stores.

PRUDENTIAL

The once-flimsy Prudential Mutual Funds is becoming solid as a rock, thanks to the hiring of some top-flight managers who have the positive goal of putting together a quality fund family. Whether this can actually be done in the brokerage house environment remains to be seen. Prudential has never been a really bad fund family and never suffered the embarrassments of some competitors, but it has certainly lacked direction. Its domestic stock funds are looking good these days, especially its utility fund. This load family's goal is to be a bit more ambitious with its funds than, say, Merrill Lynch. It prefers funds with some character, not simply pedestrian choices that won't disappoint anyone too much.

It's a mistake for Prudential not to offer a single growth and income fund, because that's something most investors demand these days. It has styles of funds that could be called growth and income, but they're all characterized as something else. In philosophy, both Prudential and Merrill Lynch are on the value side of the investment equation, while the emphasis at Dean Witter is growth.

IDS

Look quickly and carefully. The IDS Group tends to fly under the radar screens of many investors because its funds have been sold only by salespeople of the IDS financial services firm. In addition, there's been nothing particularly noteworthy about this load group other than the success of its New Dimensions fund over an extended period of time under a couple of different managers. The company also seems to have had some trouble keeping its best managers. Several of its funds that were at the top of the charts in the 1980s experienced weakness in the 1990s, though it does have a quality product line and it doesn't have to worry about hiding any skeletons in its closet.

To its credit, IDS has been intelligent about putting out long-term products. But it's not particularly press-savvy, and tends to expect everyone to write exactly what its staff says, rather than relate what the facts may be. There's no real reason to seek out IDS funds, but if your company told you that your 401(k) plan was with the IDS Group, you'd have no particular reason to rebel either.

T. ROWE PRICE

A classy group with a solid reputation and admirable performance numbers in the 1990s, T. Rowe Price Funds has increased its investment research staff. It is a very user-friendly no-load fund company. Much like what a no-load Putnam might be, it boasts above-average strength in numerous areas such as value, growth, international, municipal, and taxable fixed-income. The company tries to do the right things across the board, with a good risk-to-reward basis in its products, and a vehicle to meet just about every conceivable market. While lower in cost than Fidelity, T. Rowe Price isn't as inexpensive as Vanguard.

If an investor had his 401(k) plan set up with T. Rowe Price, there would really be no funds to avoid or any problem areas to be concerned about. T. Rowe Price funds have always done what they say, with the very small exception of its adjustable-rate mortgage (ARM) fund, which included derivatives.

FEDERATED

Designed to play with the big boys rather than the average Joe. Federated Funds, best known as an institutional money manager selling funds to bank trust departments rather than for its retail business, favors a conservative, blue-chip investment strategy. It offers a rather unexciting lineup, although its popular high-yield bond fund has done extremely well. Although it offers mostly load funds, it also has some no-loads as well.

TWENTIETH CENTURY

Presto, chango! The Twentieth Century Family of Funds has been transformed from a growth stock boutique to a full-fledged diversified fund family. That's due in large part to the addition of the Benham bond funds, especially well-known for their zero-coupon bond vehicles, but there has also been a successful launch of internally generated value and international funds. This no-load firm's roots are high-octane growth funds that remain fully invested in the stock market at all times. That makes Twentieth Century a real bull market champion. The problem in the past, however, was that all of its funds would look great or terrible at the same time, based on how the financial markets were treating growth stocks. Yet, although this fund family is a bit odd in its stance at times, it always does put the best interests of its investors first and foremost. That's a plus.

ALLIANCE CAPITAL

Consider it a money magnet. Alliance Capital Group is splendid at attracting assets, both on the institutional side where it has a great reputation for running stock fund money, and on the retail side where its hot bond concepts have garnered good and bad attention. Alliance frequently comes out with products that Merrill Lynch brokers sell in large quantitites. This load fund group has two distinct arms, the first consisting of the conservative, well-managed funds from Equitable and the other its gimmicky bond funds that do not come through Equitable.

There's reason to be cautious in considering its offerings. For example, Alliance invented the short-term world income fund, took in a huge amount of assets with the concept, and lost most of the money. It also came up with the North American government fund concept, took in an enormous amount of money, and then lost most of it. Meanwhile, its aggressively run municipal bond funds excel in bull markets and are hammered in down markets. Morningstar has found that investors often don't use the Alliance funds very well.

VAN KAMPEN AMERICAN CAPITAL

This marriage of convenience wasn't exactly made in heaven. Van Kampen American Capital is the result of the merger of two rather mediocre fund families, Van Kampen Merritt and American Capital. American Capital was primarily a stock fund family that did quite well in the 1970s but struggled throughout the 1980s. At the end of the 1980s it was wise enough to clean house, bringing in a new crop of people, who have been producing steady fund results in the 1990s. These load funds are tightly constrained in how they can invest, meaning there's little room for creativity but they're unlikely to get into a lot of trouble either. Because of the problems of the 1980s, American Capital didn't build the strong brand name recognition of worthy competitors such as Putnam or Franklin.

The merger with Van Kampen Merritt was designed to strengthen the company's position through the addition of a fixed-income shop. Van Kampen Merritt's products hadn't been all that bad, but just didn't have enough pizzazz to beat the competition. Furthermore, it was limited in its resources and offered very few stock funds. Yet the fact that the combined entity now has the bulk and potential to be a dangerous competitor and strong fund family in the next decade was underscored by its purchase by Wall Street's prestigious Morgan Stanley Group Inc. in mid-1996 for $745 million. Morgan Stanley, seeking a retail presence, was able to buy assets that included no "problem" funds. This was a sensible move that should pay off.

KEMPER

This growth-oriented fund group that sports a terrific brand name lost considerable ground over the past several years after prospering in the 1989–91 period in which growth strategies dominated the market. The strength of value investing in the 1990s left Kemper funds out in the cold in terms of performance, and the fact that the fund group was up for sale took a toll on employee morale. Some top managers were lost to other fund families during this unsettling period, though the ownership situation has now been settled with its purchase by Zurich Insurance Group. Boosting the franchise's appeal was the recent purchase of the well-known Dreman funds, which espouse a value approach.

Because Kemper's name to most individuals has become synonymous with investing, thanks to the early popularity of its money market fund and publicity surrounding its golf tournament, no scarring occurred at this load family that can't be overcome.

JANUS

A great no-load organization with high-quality growth funds, the Janus Funds should be commended for having the good sense to back off from that particular strategy when growth stocks aren't in favor. It will often move to a greater cash position or other types of stocks during those periods. The company's funds were sleepy throughout much of the 1980s but took off in 1989–91 as great results in growth stocks helped attract assets. While it has added international stocks to its lists of funds, it still doesn't try to be all things to all people. That's an intelligent approach.

STRONG

One of Morningstar's favorite fund families, it is the brain-child of savvy manager Dick Strong. The real making of this organization took place in the 1980s when Strong was heavily involved in the managing of all the funds. But Strong was hit hard by the junk bond market in 1989 when merger and acquisition activity declined dramatically. An emphasis on M&A strategy had permeated his funds at that time. Deciding to apply the brakes, Strong realized he couldn't run the firm and run all its funds as well. He began to bring in outsiders and give them autonomy. Key portfolio managers as well as company managers were put in place.

Now Strong himself runs the Strong Discovery Fund. This no-load firm is adept at both fixed-income and equity management. One problem is that it has no great value fund, though it is likely to add that to its lineup in the future. Expect Strong to expand rapidly in the 401(k) retirement account business.

SCUDDER

Best known for its international funds and its closed-end single-country funds, Scudder Funds was one of the earliest no-load fund families. It is a high-quality group with good funds but does not have a great vision for its domestic stock efforts. One problem with the firm is its rather odd corporate structure, with its headquarters and back office in Boston, managers in New York, and regional offices around the country. This was originally put in place to reach high-net-worth individuals, but this sometimes results in a lack of coherent communication among its various entities.

GRADING STOCK FUNDS BY FAMILY

The single most important factor in selecting a fund family is the quality of its domestic stock funds, Morningstar believes. Diversified U.S. equity funds—growth, growth and income, small-company, aggressive-growth, and equity-income funds—anchor long-term portfolios. Furthermore, the performance differences among domestic stock funds are more extreme than those of other fund types, such as bonds and money market funds.

To determine which of the largest fund families have the best domestic stock prowess, Morningstar graded the performance over a ten-year period, also taking into account their three- and five-year returns. It excluded those fund families that didn't have sufficiently broad product lines (meaning that it had fewer than three nonindex domestic stock funds a decade ago or fewer than six funds now). Other fund groups were moved up into their places as a result. To formulate its grades, Morningstar examined the trailing three-, five-, and ten-year periods through 1994. It then averaged returns for each family's U.S. diversified equity funds, giving a 50 percent weighting to a family's ten-year numbers, 30 percent for its five-year figure, and 20 percent for its three-year totals. In terms of risk, matters were simplified by using just the average three-year risk score. Each family's performance and risk scores were then compared with those of the U.S. diversified fund average in order to come up with letter grades ranging from A to F.

The final step was to assign each family an overall grade taking performance and risk into account.

Drum roll, please. Fidelity and American Funds, two families with significantly different investment styles, scored the highest grades of A+ and A– respectively. In the B category were Putnam, Twentieth Century, AIM, T. Rowe Price, and Franklin Templeton. Pulling a gentleman's C were Oppenheimer, MFS, Vanguard, IDS, and Merrill Lynch. While not threatening the leaders, those organizations do well enough to be viable single-fund-family candidates because all offer at least a few fine funds and enough diversity to permit the creation of balanced portfolios.

Meanwhile, D grades were assigned to Dreyfus, Smith Barney, and Dean Witter. Yet even the weakest of these families earn passing grades. While size doesn't guarantee excellence, it does mean that expenses won't move much past 2 percent, management will show some professionalism, and inflation will likely be beaten in decent market conditions. Those factors explain the appeal of investing with the major firms.

Here's a synopsis of domestic stock fund results for key families:

- Fidelity, overall grade of A+, performance A+, risk A–. "Showing no sign of slowing."
- American Funds, overall grade of A–, performance B+, risk A. "Only missing the small-cap market."
- Putnam, overall grade of B+, performance A–, risk C. "Deep and on the rise."
- Twentieth Century, overall grade of B, performance A, risk F. "Diversifying and on the rise."
- AIM, overall grade of B, performance A–, risk D+. "Up-and-comer that lacks depth."
- T. Rowe Price, overall grade of B, performance B–, risk A–. "Mediocre in the 1980s, great in the 1990s."
- Franklin Templeton, overall grade of B–, performance B–, risk A–. "A real sleeper expanding rapidly."

- Oppenheimer, overall grade of C+, performance B, risk C−. "Improving but not yet top tier."
- MFS, overall grade of C+, performance B+, risk D+. "Reliable growth stock house."
- Vanguard, overall grade of C+, performance C, risk B. "Better with balanced and bond funds."
- IDS, overall grade of C+, performance B−, risk C. "Hurt by consumer growth stocks."
- Merrill Lynch, overall grade of C, performance C−, risk B. "Best results in value markets."
- Dreyfus, overall grade of D+, performance D, risk C+. "Still hasn't found a game plan."
- Smith Barney, overall grade of D+, performance D+, risk C. "This *after* folding its worst funds!"
- Dean Witter, overall grade of D, performance D, risk D. "It's been a long, long drought."

Those are the established vintners in the mutual fund industry. Many of the most exciting funds these days actually come from the smaller fund families. They usually make no attempt to have all the necessary tools for a complete investment program, instead favoring one basic philosophy with several different shadings. It requires more work to seek out some of these funds, although the effort can be well worth it.

In all cases, the proof of the wine is in the tasting, not on the label.

CHAPTER 7

■

CHARGING AT WINDMILLS

"It is easy to see," replied Don Quixote, "that you are not used to this business of adventures. Those are giants, and if you are afraid, away with you out of here and betake your-self to prayer, while I engage them in fierce and unequal combat."

—FROM *The Ingenious Don Quixote of La Mancha*, MIGUEL DE CERVANTES

A newspaper advertisement in early 1993 fired the first volley in what was to become a year-long legal battle.

"The Pilgrim Group is proud to announce the final 1992 Mutual Fund Rankings," the ad's headline proclaimed. Those words were followed by tombstone-like award plaques with the following inscriptions:

#1 Pilgrim Adjustable Rate Securities Trust III
#2 Pilgrim Adjustable Rate Securities Trust II
#3 Pilgrim Adjustable Rate Securities Trust I
#4 Pilgrim GNMA Fund
#5 Pilgrim Regional BankShares

Investors were urged to "find out more about how this unprecedented performance can work for you." Five days after the first ad, Pilgrim ran a similar one listing those five rankings again with the headline: "Has anything like this ever happened before?"

An investor reading the advertisement would deduce that Pilgrim dominated the mutual fund charts, managing the five top-performing funds. This was untrue. None of Pilgrim's open-end mutual funds had even placed in the top 100 of all funds, and several had suffered dismal declines. The advertisement layout suggested that the first-through fifth-place rankings were related to one another and that Pilgrim held the top five slots in some uniform ranking. That wasn't the case. Only in the ad's small print was it revealed those rankings were independent of one another, each determined by a fund's showing in an entirely different category that was formulated by Pilgrim. The fact Pilgrim scored a 1, 2, or 3 here, or a 4 there, and a 5 somewhere else was simply a numerical curiosity, not evidence of any superior combined performance.

The commentary published in *Morningstar Mutual Funds* every two weeks has been the pulpit from which the company has taken many of its strongest stands on controversial issues.

The Pilgrim ad was the target in a February 19, 1993, commentary written by Don Phillips, entitled "Lies, Damned Lies, and Fund Advertisements" (the "lies, damned lies" an allusion to American humorist Mark Twain's wry comments on the misuse of statistics). It led with the statement: "Mutual fund advertising has hit a new low." It

added: "That Pilgrim could twist its often-poor performance record to create marketing material that makes it
look like the industry's most successful manager presents an
important lesson in the use and abuse of statistics in the
fund industry today."

Pilgrim fired back with its lawyers. First came an irate
warning letter from its headquarters in Los Angeles, followed by numerous faxes from New York law firms threatening legal action if the comments weren't retracted.
Morningstar did print a clarification of its intent, in which
it also stood by all of its commentary points. But that didn't
assuage anyone. The fund company filed a lawsuit in
California Superior Court on March 18, 1993, accusing
Morningstar of "falsely imputing to Pilgrim Group actions
and statements" it did not make, seeking $2 million in
compensatory damages. It cited a "flagrantly libelous article
which set forth a scathing and wholly unfounded attack"
on the group. The complainant said there was nothing
inaccurate in the ads.

In its legal response, Morningstar noted Pilgrim had
failed to identify "a single statement in the commentary
which Pilgrim claims is false," and asserted that libel laws
protect Morningstar in light of the absence of "provably
false factual assertions." Morningstar asked the court to dismiss the suit, and when Judge David Yaffe refused, the
company appealed to the California Court of Appeals and
eventually to the state Supreme Court. The Supreme Court
ordered the Court of Appeals to hear arguments on the
merit of the suit, which it did in December 1993.

The eventual ruling went Morningstar's way. The
court's decision to dismiss the Pilgrim suit was made public March 19, 1994, a full year after the initial lawsuit was
filed. The judges said in the ruling that Morningstar's commentary was a "timely expression of opinion on a matter of
public concern." They called it "precisely the kind of
speech which the First Amendment is designed to protect."

The National Association of Securities Dealers eventually slapped sanctions on Pilgrim and its chairman, Palomba Weingarten, for the advertisements. But it didn't do so until more than a year and seven months after they were printed, and seven months after the Morningstar libel suit had been thrown out of court. According to documents obtained from the NASD, on October 26, 1994, Weingarten was censured, fined $25,000, and suspended from associating with any NASD member in a principal capacity for three months. The suspension order stated that Pilgrim, acting through Weingarten, published newspaper advertisements that "contained misleading or exaggerated statements and failed to file the advertisements with the NASD within 10 days of the first use of the advertisements as required." But there was a far greater toll on Pilgrim than that. A conservative estimate is that it had spent more than $100,000 on legal fees to pursue the libel suit. It subsequently sold off most of its funds, keeping only adjustable-rate mortgage funds and two short-term world income funds, renamed the Astra Funds.

The NASD revised its advertising standards as a result of the controversy to make the presentations more uniform, with legal warnings and standardized time periods required for all funds that are advertised. One persistent problem, unfortunately, is that NASD rules don't apply to those funds which aren't its members, and some nonmember funds still have a tendency to be less than straightforward in their ads.

WHO'S IN CHARGE

Disclosure has come slowly to some aspects of the fund industry.

On September 22, 1989, a Morningstar commentary bemoaned the fact that for seventeen years the SEC and the mutual fund industry hadn't been able to come to an agree-

ment requiring that a fund disclose the names of its portfolio managers in its prospectus. The primary reason given
by fund executives at that time for fighting the disclosure
was that they didn't want to support the star system in
which investors buy and sell funds based on managers,
rather than the fund companies.

The commentary pointed out that publicly traded companies were required to list their top managers, and that
fund managers certainly wouldn't buy a stock in a company that didn't comply with this basic regulation. Fund
investors are "not little children," the piece asserted, and do
not need to be sheltered from information because someone thinks they might misuse it. "It's important to realize
the credibility of the fund industry is under question with
this issue," it said. "If mutual fund companies persist in
defending a seemingly indefensible position, they may
jeopardize their most valuable asset—the public trust."

Four years later, disclosure of portfolio manager names
was finally mandated by the SEC.

GRADING SHAREHOLDER REPORTS

The wrapper does make a difference.

Throughout the late 1980s, Morningstar noted that
many shareholder reports gave little pertinent information
to investors about the fund in question. So it became the
first to grade shareholder reports, issuing marks ranging
from A to F, which became a regular feature in *Morningstar
Mutual Funds*. After explaining this new feature to subscribers, Morningstar set out to test the accuracy of its
hypothesis that concern for shareholders demonstrated in a
fund's reporting carries over into other, more pertinent
investment aspects.

In its September 21, 1990, commentary entitled "You Can Judge a Book by Its Cover," it listed shareholder report grades for 100 major fund groups. Most that received high marks also had produced superior investment results for their customers, it found. Solid-performing funds generally have nothing to hide. Interestingly, funds with the worst grades also tended to have the highest expense ratios for their funds. The investor obviously was not high on their list of priorities.

Receiving As for their reports were funds such as Clipper, Parnassus, Primary Trend, Sequoia, Acorn, Brandywine, Evergreen, Gabelli, Merrill Lynch, Strong, Vanguard, Blanchard, and T. Rowe Price. Meanwhile, others such as Franklin, Shearson Lehman, and Eaton Vance received poor marks. Fidelity's had been only so-so. However, Morningstar noted recently that both Franklin and Fidelity have since gotten better.

"While there are some quality firms that issue poor reports, the overall evidence overwhelmingly suggests that investors will significantly upgrade their investments by restricting their choices to fund companies that offer high-quality reports," it was noted. Investors can freely choose to invest with a fund company that neglects their concerns and turns the shareholder report into meaningless paper or a marketing device. On the other hand, they can opt for a fund management company that treats them with the respect they deserve as owners of the fund.

NO CRYSTAL BALL

Beware gurus bearing forecasts.

Though no one can completely generalize about "good" and "bad" strategies, funds that profess to have a crystal ball behind their investing and stake their fortunes on the ability to predict major events are usually doomed to failure.

They typically lay claim to economic, interest rate, or market sector trends, emphasizing broad topics over smaller, specific issues. They are also promoted loudly by their fund companies, who push the soothsayer in charge to the forefront of media attention. In the commentary "The Questions Worth Asking" in the September 4, 1992, *Morningstar Mutual Funds,* John Rekenthaler deduced that most funds which seek to hitch their wagons to bold, sweeping fund strategies get great press in the short run and spotty results in the long run.

For example, Elaine Garzarelli, who earned a reputation for her exhaustive research reports and is best known for having accurately called the 1987 stock market crash, enjoyed the limelight as her two-month-old Shearson Sector Analysis Fund actually gained ground on Black Monday. Comstock Partners, led by former Merrill Lynch prognosticator Stanley Salvigsen, guided the Dreyfus Capital Value Fund to nearly as good a performance. Garzarelli was seen everywhere in newspaper, magazine, and television features. The high-visibility Salvigsen and his partners were spotlighted in a number of *Barron's* interviews on the market's prospects. Both of these funds received a rush of incoming money after their 1987 successes, quickly leaping past the $500 million mark.

But that's where the excitement ended, as both funds tumbled in 1988 and suffered choppy results thereafter. Both Garzarelli and her fund were phased out by her company, and she is now happily doing economic and market research and money management with two firms bearing her name. Despite her mutual fund misadventure, Garzarelli is still able to grab Wall Street's attention with her pronouncements on overall market trends. The other fund, Dreyfus Capital Value, has turned in dismal returns except for its strong performance in 1989. Other high-visibility failures in the fund business that were run by people who supposedly knew more than the rest of us included Wall

Street strategist Michael Sherman's Shearson Multiple Opportunities and storied economist Henry Kaufman's National Global Allocation Fund. Both were closed down due to disastrous results.

"Tune out the noise," Rekenthaler admonished investors who might be wooed by such big-picture celebrity management. "Broad-thinking managers may offer perceptive, interesting opinions, but they're unlikely to translate that knowledge into fund profits."

MAGELLAN CALLS

The bigger they are, the more the experts want them to fall.

Predicting the prospects for the biggest and most scrutinized of all stock mutual funds, the $50 billion-plus Fidelity Magellan, has become a national obsession. Morningstar's advice has run counter to the army of nay-sayers who felt the fund would completely give up the ghost once the legendary manager Peter Lynch stepped down.

The individual that Fidelity has in charge of the mighty Magellan at a given time, Morningstar contends, will always be someone carefully chosen because of his or her self-confidence and proven ability to make savvy investment decisions. The fact that there is only one Peter Lynch does not doom a fund forever, any more than the fact there was only one Babe Ruth doomed the New York Yankees. A Mickey Mantle, Reggie Jackson, or Don Mattingly may be right around the corner. Like the Yankees of old, Fidelity has quite a farm team to draw upon.

Throughout Magellan's history, but particularly toward the end of Lynch's lengthy tenure, during the relatively short stewardship of Morris Smith, throughout Jeff Vinik's four-year leadership, and since Robert Stansky's selection in May of 1996, many experts have been bearish on the fund. Yet Morningstar maintained that the fund could continue to have above-average long-term performance as Fidelity Investments made sure its flagship would always have the best available captain. In Lynch's later days at the helm, critics claimed that its enormous bulk meant that it had become too large to outperform the market. Not so, said Morningstar, for the fund neither looked nor acted like the Standard & Poor's 500, and utilized its own unique philosophy to beat that benchmark handily. Some pundits charged that Lynch was just lucky, while others viewed him as a once-in-a-lifetime genius who could never remotely be replaced. Morningstar argued that such viewpoints overlooked the strong odds that within Fidelity's impressive stable of talent a suitable new direction could be found. There are, after all, many ways to run a Magellan.

As Morris Smith took over Magellan in mid-1990, a weekly table in a Boston newspaper compared Magellan's short-term results with those of the S&P 500. The feature lost much of its appeal as Smith's slow start was transformed into a sharp rebound in late 1990 and throughout 1991. Morningstar had already informed its subscribers that in Smith's five years at Fidelity OTC, he had been known for his dependability and lack of color as he consistently beat the competition by a moderate amount. He did change the fund's overall direction in that he had a greater admiration for larger-capitalization stocks than did Lynch, but his cautious tactics of concentrating on proven growth stocks in health care and other consumer staples fit perfectly with market sentiment during that time period.

When Smith exited and Vinik took over, the new boss surprised many observers by initially replacing the Magellan's traditional consumer nondurables with energy stocks, technology companies, and plenty of cash and bonds. Critical articles lambasted Vinik for abandoning Magellan's historic principles. Yet Morningstar maintained that Vinik had previously demonstrated more flexibility than any fund manager in America since Peter Lynch, transforming a conventional group of low P/E stocks at Fidelity Contrafund into a batch of cheap small caps supplemented by a big cash holding. Then, at Fidelity Growth & Income, he'd loaded up on biotechnology and emerging-growth stocks. In both of those cases he'd boldly juggled fund charters, had high turnover rates, and deftly beat the market by Lynch-style margins.

"The fact is, Vinik follows Lynch's Magellan tradition far more closely than did Smith," said a commentary entitled "Magellan Myths" in the April 30, 1993, *Morningstar Mutual Funds*. "One must therefore admire Vinik's admirable record with some skepticism. The odds for his success are very good—but not as strong as they would be for Lynch himself." Though Vinik's first year in charge produced stellar results, his subsequent three-year return fell below that of the Standard & Poor's 500. His heavy bet on volatile technology stocks in 1995 drew nervous attention from the investment community, as did his ill-timed move into cash and bonds in the months before his departure. Vinik also made some controversial public statements, which led to Fidelity barring its fund managers from publicly discussing specific stocks.

Morningstar was never a mindless Vinik cheerleader and, for example, warned investors of his risky technology play. "While the fund should continue to be a long-term star," the analysis in *Morningstar Mutual Funds* noted, "it would be painful to buy just before a short-term drop." Yet when Vinik departed to run his own money management firm, Morningstar expressed a belief that he had perhaps been tried unfairly by many of his critics, since his overall record remained quite good. Consider the irony: The enormous Magellan was often criticized as being too big and bland. Yet when a portfolio manager tried to be more flexible and inventive, as one might do with a much smaller fund, that focus too was ridiculed.

The replacement of Vinik with Robert Stansky, who had capably run the Fidelity Growth Company Fund as a classic growth fund since 1987, provided a style that's perhaps better suited to Magellan, in Morningstar's opinion. Stansky had already demonstrated a preference for larger companies, hadn't repositioned his fund as aggressively in various sectors as Vinik had, and was generally considered more predictable and less of a risk-taker. While he's likely to be more flexible with Magellan's portfolio than he was with Fidelity Growth Company Fund, he undoubtedly will not go to the extremes that Vinik did. The assumption has been made that Stansky will stick closely with growth stocks and, while he may not necessarily remain 100 percent invested in stocks all the time, will be unlikely to jump into bonds as wholeheartedly as Vinik did. It will take a while to determine whether Stansky ran Fidelity Growth Company Fund as he did in order to adhere to its charter, or whether the same strategy will indeed be transferred to the larger Magellan.

Magellan under Stansky still has an excellent chance to be in the upper one-third of growth funds, Morningstar is convinced, but it still can't relive the explosive gains of its first decade under Lynch. Investors who expect it to rank in the top 1 percent of growth funds will be sorely disappointed, for it is no longer a small fund capable of such agile navigation. One constant, however, is that its manager will always face intense examination and, in many cases, unrealistic expectations.

INVESTOR ALERT

Always know what you own.

In the early 1990s, nervous investors made what they considered to be a logical decision and moved into the safer haven of diversified domestic stock funds emphasizing growth or growth and income. However, these began to change in composition as portfolio managers attempted to boost their returns in order to attract more assets.

The *Morningstar Investor* newsletter's March 1995 article entitled "Funds' Technology Affair Worth Close Scrutiny" by Rekenthaler explained that technology had swollen to more than 16 percent of U.S. diversified funds' equity assets—a historically high percentage and nearly twice the weighting carried by the Standard & Poor's 500. Funds with the highest total returns and greatest sales for the period had more than 20 percent of their portfolios in technology, and in cases such as Fidelity Magellan the amount was significantly higher. The bottom line, however, was that many fund investors had no clue that this radical adjustment was occurring in their holdings. "It is unlikely that most fund investors want that much technology exposure and they won't be happy the next time the technology sector heads south," the article reported, in light of the fact that technology is the market's most expensive and volatile group. "There's a good chance, in fact, that they will bail out at the first opportunity and cost themselves a lot of money."

Technology, while it is definitely capable of making money for investors, is a group that always has experienced dramatic ups and downs on its way to longer-term gains. An investor choosing a diversified fund should be made fully aware if he is accepting this inherent volatility or any other type of risk, whether it be from a stock group or derivative instruments. Always thoroughly examine a fund's actual investments if you expect to understand how it will perform. The fewer surprises, the better.

DERIVATIVE MADNESS

Morningstar's stance on the Pilgrim Group drew the attention of Washington. U.S. Representative Edward Markey, a

Massachusetts Democrat who was then chairman of the Telecommunications and Finance Subcommittee of the House Commerce Committee, described the Pilgrim advertisements in the November 8, 1993, issue of *Time* magazine as "the most egregious examples of manipulating mutual fund rankings of which I am aware."

When Don Phillips was asked to testify at a hearing before Markey's subcommittee on September 27, 1994, regarding regulatory problems facing the mutual fund industry, his presentation shifted to a newer and more dangerous threat: the dreaded D word, meaning derivative investments.

Derivatives have represented one of the greatest challenges to mutual fund investing in the 1990s. Available for more than four decades in their more "vanilla" forms, derivative instruments are basically financial instruments whose value is based on another security. They are often used as a hedge against financial and commercial risk. In and of themselves, they're neither inherently good or bad. For example, derivatives have often contained exposure to fluctuations in prices or availability of certain materials. The basic financial goal is to link an inherently unstable or negative entity to one that is much more stable and to therefore produce a financial benefit.

It was, of course, discovered that derivatives could also be used to generate positive returns, and, with some luck, wildly positive returns. Financial pressure on corporate treasurers and portfolio managers in recent years led some of them to swing for the fences by speculating in these volatile instruments, in some cases handled through traditional investment firms. A mind-boggling array of different derivative packages with a variety of names evolved. Such instruments are incredibly complex and how they function hasn't always been fully understood, in many cases even by management of some firms that put considerable money in them. Derivatives speculation ravaged many mutual funds and was blamed for the bankruptcy of Orange County in 1994 and huge losses in the investment portfolios of many mainline American companies such as Procter & Gamble.

Some of the more exotic derivatives pose a significant threat to the mutual fund industry and the general investing public, Phillips warned the panel. Making matters worse, such trading has often produced significant losses in funds that ironically had been offered to average investors as conservative, low-risk choices. The Morningstar president proposed that the industry standardize the disclosure of derivative investments and not simply relegate key information to financial footnotes. In addition, fund companies should begin to make their portfolios available on a monthly basis to the press, research organizations, and other interested groups so that independent sources could apply uniform analysis to funds, he said.

BOND BOMBS

Too many people unfortunately learn lessons the hard way—over and over again. Yet there have been some common traits among most aggressive, ill-chosen bond investments that should be kept in mind.

Mortgage derivative funds, like Ginnie Maes before them, government plus, junk bond, and short-term world income funds, all featured:

- **New strategies** that hadn't been used before.
- **An apparent free lunch** because each offered something for nothing and could therefore attract assets.
- **Complexity**, in that none of the strategies proved easy to analyze and often required access to nonpublic financial statements and sophisticated accounting knowledge.
- **Inadequate disclosure** in which fund companies failed to fill the information breach as they provided a blizzard

of information but little discussion of a fund's essential weaknesses.

The commentary "Mortgage Derivatives: The Lessons" on June 24, 1994, took a closer look at all the top bond fund bombs that have been so damaging to investors. Whether it was Ginnie Mae funds in 1986, options-writing government plus funds in 1987, junk bond funds in 1989–90, short-term world income funds in 1992, or mortgage derivative funds in 1994, each "lured the unwary with their vigor and youth" but eventually stung those same investors.

Consider mortgage derivatives, which were actually built for safety reasons because the uncertain maturity schedule of mortgage pass-throughs detracts from their value. To attack this problem, investment bankers began to repackage mortgages into a series of new issues, called collateralized mortgage obligations (CMOs). Many CMOs were engineered to obtain steadier cash flows than the original mortgages and could be sold at higher prices, which led to the creation of even more derivatives. While a mortgage's CMOs may sell for more than the price of the whole, they carry just as much risk as the original mortgage. If 90 percent of a mortgage is sliced into CMOs bearing only half the prepayment risk of the original security, the final 10 percent compensates by carrying a risk level more than five times as great as the original issue.

But these leftover CMOs, the exotics with names like interest-only, principal-only, and Z-tranche, are extremely sensitive to interest rate moves and their durations change rapidly along with rates and prepayments. Many government bond funds began to use exotics, believing they could get top returns with modest risks. Well, they could—for a while. Then funds such as Managers Intermediate Mortgage and Piper Institutional Government, which had successfully used mortgage derivatives from 1991 through 1993, suffered dramatic plunges in early 1994 when interest rates jumped sharply. Funds marketed as conservative vehicles, like PaineWebber Short-Term U.S. Government and Value Line Adjustable Rate Securities (whose name was changed to Value Line Intermediate Bond Fund in November 1995) were also hammered, with one quarter's principal losses wiping out four years' worth of their yield advantage over cash choices.

GIMMICK PLAYS

Like a money market fund—almost.

The raft of yield-oriented funds touted as money market fund substitutes got Morningstar's dander up on June 28, 1991. Its commentary "As Good as Cash?" pointed out that higher yields of so-called money market alternatives are accompanied by higher and substantially different risks than true money market funds.

Investors should always carefully assess such risks before deciding to abandon the known security of a money market fund. Some variations in adjustable-rate funds were a case in point, with some of these new products taking on greater interest rate sensitivity, while others carry greater credit risk. No matter what any salesperson may tell you, adjustable-rate funds are clearly not as interchangeable as money market funds. To be deployed effectively in a portfolio, new offerings require much greater initial inquiry by the investor and ongoing research.

Short-term multi-market funds raised additional question marks. The fancy machinations that make these funds work, such as currency hedges, interest rate swaps, and futures positions, are off-the-balance-sheet items that change rapidly. Because the plan depends on both a significant spread between currencies and the narrowing of that spread, there is always a rather limited opportunity. The true concern is always how such funds would do once the inefficiencies that they'd been able to exploit have diminished. Making matters worse, the potential in their strategies and the talent of their managers usually haven't been fully demonstrated at the time an investor is given a chance to invest.

FAST GROWTH

As the intricacies and potential problems of the mutual fund industry grow, so does the audience for research. Morningstar's entry into the field came in a decade that began with the industry holding about $95 billion in assets, which by end of the decade had grown to $982 billion.

In 1985, Morningstar's first full year of existence, the sales of $114 billion in stock and bond funds had doubled all previous annual records. Another plus for the new company was the dynamic growth of now-famous direct-marketing companies such as Fidelity Investments, Vanguard Group, Dreyfus Corp., and T. Rowe Price Associates. These targeted the investor who thought for himself and who would need information in order to effectively make choices. There was a growing number of investment choices for the investor to try to understand, with Ginnie Mae and Treasury bond funds having been introduced in 1983.

Total assets of mutual funds reached $1 trillion for the first time in January 1990 and have since grown to triple that amount as they've reached more than 9,000 funds, with no end in sight. Those who say the 1980s were "the decade of the mutual fund" had better consider updating that assessment each and every decade as we move forward through the twenty-first century. Baby-boomers planning for their own retirement and their children's educations are exceedingly comfortable with the mutual fund concept and are expected to actively use it considerably more in the future to meet their needs. They're also much more willing to stick with their funds because they understand the importance of diversity and the need to be a long-term investor. As a result, mutual funds are here to stay.

Chapter 8

■

LEGENDS

---

*"Whoever imagines that the average Wall Street profession-
al is looking for reasons to buy exciting stocks hasn't spent
much time on Wall Street. The fund manager most likely is
looking for reasons not to buy exciting stocks, so that he can
offer the proper excuses if those exciting stocks happen to
go up."*
—Legendary portfolio manager Peter
Lynch on the pitfalls of running with
the herd in his book *One Up on Wall Street*

Perhaps no group better symbolizes pop artist Andy
Warhol's concept of the modern, fleeting nature of
notoriety, in which everyone is famous for about fifteen
minutes, than mutual fund portfolio managers. The
Morningstar rankings of total returns place these professional money-managers in a neat pecking order

announced at regular intervals. Journalists interview those who sit atop a particular category's perch for a given quarter or year, seeking to glean some of their investment wisdom.

The excitement of those who nail down a high position among the thousands of potential manager candidates is obvious. They're enthusiastic and ready to talk, knowing that their efforts will be rewarded with new fund assets, general prestige, and, more than likely, a bigger paycheck from their employer. Alas, those who are so anointed seldom enjoy a long tenure in the limelight. Their latest results are soon forgotten and there's tomorrow to worry about once again. They're replaced by new pretenders to the throne, the result of rapidly changing economic and market events that chew up one investment strategy after another.

But enduring beyond a given year's all-stars are the true legends of the mutual fund game. They are the Michael Jordans and Joe Montanas of their field. Having had the opportunity to personally interview many of these legends, I've found that their work not only holds up, but, if anything, looms even larger as time passes. They are discussed admiringly by their peers. In some cases they have been true pioneers, while in others they have beaten their competitors on a consistent long-term basis. Others often seek to copy their successes by carefully emulating their strategies in a studied by-the-numbers fashion that almost never works.

The big three of the mutual fund portfolio manager hierarchy are most assuredly Sir John Templeton, founder of the Templeton Funds, which opened Americans' eyes to world investing; Peter Lynch, star manager of the giant Fidelity Magellan Fund, which rode an eclectic style to great profit for its investors; and John Neff, who piloted the huge Vanguard Windsor Fund using a consistent value formula that emphasized the income attributes of stocks. All three of these men have retired from active management, Neff most recently, but their exploits and their ideas permeate not only their own organizations, but many other fund companies as well. In addition to this august trio, a number of other legendary managers fill out a top ten constructed by Morningstar, a company whose staffers have more contact with key portfolio managers and their records than just about anyone else does. It's obvious from comparing these winners' varied game plans that there are many different ways to become a triumphant portfolio manager.

Here are, from Morningstar's vantage point, the top ten mutual fund portfolio managers of all time (the final seven are listed in alphabetical order):

TOP ALL-TIME MANAGER NO. 1: SIR JOHN TEMPLETON

World-renowned value investor Templeton started his first fund in 1954 and immediately became a pioneer and trend-setter. Beyond being a gifted value manager, Templeton saw early on and more vividly than other managers that the world's economy was truly a global one. He started investing aggressively in areas outside the United States, including Japan. He took the U.S. securities valuation approach and applied it to other markets, enabling him, for example, to compare Japanese companies to European and U.S. firms. This greatly enlarged the pool from which he could find discount companies selling at great prices. By doing this so early, making cross-border comparisons before anyone else considered it, he uncovered all sorts of market inefficiencies in world markets and was able to deliver a remarkable return to investors over an extended period of time.

Templeton was also shrewd in determining that mutual fund companies would become very big business one day. He prospered by buying the publicly traded stock of many of these fund companies when their prices were deeply depressed following the Wall Street crash of 1987. Keep in mind that some prognosticators of the day were saying that the Dow Jones industrial average could plummet as low as 400 and that terrible equity returns would be the norm for decades. By boldly stepping up to the plate, Templeton made big money for his investors. He has, however, always seen the big picture. A fine public speaker, Templeton often delivers a presentation in which he describes a terrible economic scenario of depressions, wars, recessions, and calamities of all types. He then explains that he's been describing the twentieth century, which has also been a time of phenomenally high investment returns.

His value theme is deep within all of the Templeton Funds, which are now a part of the Franklin Templeton Group. Because all of its funds look to buy securities at good valuation levels, the differences between them are predominately geographic, such as whether a fund includes the U.S. market or not. Even a small-company fund of Templeton's will espouse the same value beliefs and won't go chasing after the latest high-flyers. Templeton brought a classic, textbook, American value-oriented fundamental analysis to a global landscape. More fund companies and investors think globally today because of all the advance work by the visionary John Templeton.

TOP ALL-TIME MANAGER NO. 2: PETER LYNCH

As the first high-visibility portfolio manager superstar, Lynch achieved greatness with the Fidelity Magellan Fund by not following any one set investment philosophy. Instead, he had an almost chameleon-like ability to scrutinize different stocks from completely different angles and to appreciate the positive attributes that assorted types of investors would see in them. Lynch has had an uncanny ability to wear a value investor's hat when he looks at one company's situation and then wear a growth investor's hat when he looks at another. It is the ability to know when to wear which hat, and how to apply the correct analysis, that made his investment style so successful over an extended period of time.

Lynch has written books and magazine articles, and delivered countless talks and interviews on investing, but this common touch doesn't make him any easier to pigeonhole into one style because he never does anything that could be considered formulaic. Consider some of his classic investments. He took a big position in long-term bonds in the early 1980s when interest rates were peaking and rode them a long distance. He took a big stock position in Chrysler Corp. when it was on the verge of bankruptcy. These represent two very different types of disciplines. The ability to bet on interest rates and the relative value of bonds versus stocks represents asset allocation savvy. Going into a deeply distressed company, seeing the value in it, and betting on a turnaround situation is pure fundamental analysis. Adding to his diversity of style, Lynch also owned plenty of classic growth companies in his portfolio. That agility and mental toughness is why many other portfolio managers admire him and consider him to be a "manager's manager."

His message to investors is to not forsake common sense, to develop your own opinions about products and services, and to harness all of your senses and abilities when considering a company and its stock. Never ignore knowledge you may have derived as a consumer of various products and never blindly accept numbers and analysis as reasons to buy any stock. It's unlikely that Lynch ever totally bought into the technological screen capacities of Fidelity Investments, since his own mind processed masses of information so rapidly that it was less necessary for him to do so. Some might argue this approach would hinder him today if he were running large sums of money, but that, of course, is mere speculation. What Lynch was known for was talking to all sorts of company management, taking numerous trips to visit companies, and for poring over all sorts of company annual reports. What he was often looking for was the intangibiles, those nameless items that put different weightings and different criteria to investments than what a computer would come up with. In many ways, Lynch was a maverick who refused to look at anything in conventional terms.

Lynch in his heyday as manager did complain about the growing size of Magellan, comparing its asset size in the 1980s at various times to the economies of certain European countries. After thirteen years of running the fund, he retired from managing in 1990 at a relatively early age. But his dramatic investment results make a compelling case for the argument that active management, rather than simply indexing stocks, can add sufficient value to overcome any fund fees. Lynch's theories and philosophies on investing percolate throughout the Fidelity Investments system and its managers routinely talk about what Peter Lynch did, says, or has encouraged with his words. The basic message: Keep looking at all situations, continue to turn over all of the rocks, and know when to apply the right criteria in the right situation.

TOP ALL-TIME MANAGER NO. 3: JOHN NEFF

Neff is a premier value-oriented investor who built the mighty Vanguard Windsor Fund using a concentrated portfolio that usually invested in larger-capitalization stocks during his thirty-one years at the helm. He had astute insight into the money management process, determining that if investors want income, they buy bonds, while if they want growth, they buy stocks. Because of those separate goals, investors who buy stocks systematically undervalue the income component of stocks, Neff discovered. As a result, those investors almost always undervalue the income component of equity, which in the longer run can actually be a substantial element of the total return from stocks.

Extending his logic, Neff would employ some basic mathematics to analyze stocks and their price-to-earnings. The expected growth rate and relative price can provide a barometer of how expensive your purchase actually is, he found. If you buy those that are cheap using that guideline and also have considerable income potential, you have obtained great downside protection and substantial upside potential as well. He was so focused on yield and growth prospects relative to price that he was constantly buying stocks in cheaper areas of the market. For the most part, he was indifferent to where he found these values. But while he had no profound like or dislike for any one section of the market, undervalued choices tended to be in the more mundane industries. Autos and financial services were groups he loved through the years and played very effectively, mostly because they met his criteria quite well. In some cases, as much as three-fourths of his portfolio might be in stocks from those two areas. When he concentrated in certain sectors, it wasn't that he loved those sectors, but rather that he believed in his basic valuation model so much that he was willing to follow it wherever it led him.

Neff never had as high a profile as Lynch. One never felt that he enjoyed being interviewed by journalists all that much, while Lynch was much more willing to take time out to play the role of teacher. But there were other reasons that extended beyond the fact that he wasn't as outgoing a fellow. For one thing, the giant Windsor was always smaller than the truly gigantic Magellan and Lynch therefore drew most of the scrutiny. Windsor was also closed to new investors for a few years. Furthermore, Lynch's fund wasn't as concentrated and there was more interest in following his moves with many "discovered" new stocks than the less flashy holdings of Neff, who was generally dealing in big-name companies like Ford Motor Co. and General Motors. But Neff's ongoing legacy is his appreciation of the yield component in stocks. Though underprized by investors and often ignored, it is the more steady component of total return and can lead to significant improvement in long-term returns with less risk. It's a lesson worth learning.

TOP ALL-TIME MANAGER NO. 4:
SHELBY DAVIS

Like Peter Lynch, Shelby Davis is a portfolio manager with the strong respect of his peers. His particular investment combination of growth and value has reflected a number of themes in the Davis New York Venture Fund he has managed since 1969. For instance, he invested in energy-related companies in the 1970s, interest-rate-sensitive companies and brand name goods companies in the 1980s, and financial services firms in the 1990s when other managers weren't perceptive enough to be doing the same. After the financial boom of the 1980s, many experts felt the money had already been made in financial services. Davis instead envisioned even more growth, as Americans moved from a spending to a savings mode, and massive demographic trends signaled more and more investment. He also foresaw the opportunities in consumer staples companies based on foreign exposure and new consumers coming from faraway places such as China and Russia.

Davis basically spots big trends from simple observations and deftly translates them into ways to make money. All of the information is available for others to see, but his grasp of it is perceptive and unique. The key has been consistency of return, not running hot or cold, but providing a wonderful ride for investors who find that their faith in him has been more than justified. His avoidance of risk certainly has kept a lot of investors on board. When you assess the best returns for a given decade, too often the ride has been so volatile in some funds that shaken investors leave and never derive the full benefit. That's definitely not the case with one of the smooth-sailing funds of Davis Selected Advisers.

TOP ALL-TIME MANAGER NO. 5: JEAN-MARIE EVEILLARD

Unconventional. Diverse. Spectacularly successful. Those words describe the style of portfolio manager Jean-Marie Eveillard, a native of France who's willing to look anywhere around the globe at virtually any type of investment that strikes his fancy. He may be one of the only portfolio managers who does not have a computer terminal in his office, although he has plenty of people right outside his office who do have them. This risk-conscious, globally focused value investor has delivered the very steadiest performance in his SoGen International Fund since he began managing it in 1979.

Basic components in Eveillard's portfolio have been domestic stocks, foreign stocks, and gold, with additional holdings in domestic cash, international bonds, and a variety of other instruments that make every other mutual fund in America seem like a sector fund. Its fifteen-year performance has been remarkably similar to that of the Standard & Poor's 500, but at a fraction of the volatility. Considering that it rarely has more than half of its assets in stocks, delivering a return equal to the S&P 500 during one of its most bullish time periods with little risk is a mind-boggling accomplishment. This is another manager whose investors stay on board for the long ride, not worrying whether it makes the top spot in fund performance in a given quarter or year. To come up with a truly unique style in the maze of funds currently offered today is remarkable. Eveillard and his fund are both one of a kind.

TOP ALL-TIME MANAGER NO. 6: KEN HEEBNER

A classic stock-picker who has won the admiration of money-managers everywhere, Heebner does exactly what he wants when he wants to do it and makes no attempt whatsoever to conform to any generally accepted rules of management. Few managers in the fund business are in a position to do that in the modern marketplace. He might put his entire portfolio into ten stocks if he wants, or put 60 percent of his fund's assets into a given sector if that's where he sees an opportunity. Because Heebner has a reputation for moving in and out of stocks very suddenly, his nickname among rival managers is "Big Foot." Even if in the process he pushes the stock down momentarily, once he's made up his mind, he's gone.

Though Heebner has capably run a number of the New England and the Capital Growth Management funds, the CGM Capital Developments Fund, which he has managed since 1977, may be the best showcase of his talents. Closed to new investors since the mid-1980s and therefore relatively small with about $500 million in assets, it has an excellent long-term track record with virtually all of those assets derived from capital appreciation. In 1991, the fund was up an amazing 99 percent. He has a willingness to make huge bets on individual market sectors and has effectively played a number of cyclical companies, such as the airlines. Obviously, this aggressive, eclectic management style can mean a volatile flight for investors on the way to its strong returns.

TOP ALL-TIME MANAGER NO. 7: MARK MOBIUS

This rigorously trained value investor with international experience fit well into the Templeton organization when he joined it as manager of its Far East division in 1987, but he also elevated it to a new level. He boldly pushed beyond the more established foreign countries that John Templeton had pioneered into the smaller, emerging markets where no other portfolio manager had ventured before. While other fund companies have since moved into these markets, no one knows as much about them as Mobius, who has amassed more than twenty years' worth of important contacts. He spends long days on the move visiting factories, listening to company stories, and observing trends around the globe. Though based in Hong Kong, he's as likely to be in Latin America or Eastern Europe as he tirelessly seeks out companies for investment. The manager of several top Templeton funds such as Templeton Developing Markets Trust, he's also responsible for Templeton's pioneering efforts with new funds in Vietnam and in Russia.

Mobius brings a prudent investment attitude to a highly speculative investment arena. He often relates, for example, the story of a company he visited at the bottom of a mountain that told him its factory was at the top of the mountain and therefore not worth visiting. No investor had ever asked to see the factory before, but Mobius insisted on going all the way to the top of the mountain to take a look. Turns out he discovered nothing but an empty building, which was hardly what was promised. In regions where key financial information is not readily available, such a willingness to perform legwork and do basic research is a major plus.

TOP ALL-TIME MANAGER NO. 8: MICHAEL PRICE

An intricate knowledge of bankruptcies and turnaround situations is what sets Michael Price apart from other value investors such as John Templeton or John Neff. Not all of the stocks he owns are of companies in such dire straits, but the skills derived from that extreme form of value investing influence all of the funds that Price runs. Besides understanding the likely legal and financial proceedings and what's to be salvaged from a firm where everything has gone bad, he can determine the core value of any business and how much an outsider would be willing to pay for it. He can put a very accurate value on any business, compare it to the current stock price, and figure how many cents on the dollar are being paid to buy the company today versus its fundamental value.

The excellent investment track records of the Mutual Series funds since he began running them in 1975 is based on identifying the "right" companies trading at 50 cents on the dollar and avoiding others that are more expensive. All of this ironically makes for low-risk funds, even though many investors panic whenever they even hear the word "bankruptcy." Bankruptcy, you see, is actually a tremendous investment opportunity for someone who knows the turf. There are many aspects to it, and sometimes debt securities may be purchased rather than common stock. A number of money-managers who own stock in a company that goes into receivership are forced to sell because part of their prudency is not owning companies in bankruptcy. This kind of artificial and forced rule can create inefficiency in the marketplace, while creating an opportunity for someone like Price. He makes money doing something different, and it works. As a result, more funds will likely try to copy his approach.

The most dramatic indication of Price's professional talent and industrywide respect came in mid-1995 when Franklin Templeton agreed to buy his Heine Securities, which manages the Mutual Series funds. The sale price of more than $500 million included five-year employment contracts for Price and his five key managers. Obviously, Franklin Templeton was buying more than just a famous fund name. It wanted Michael Price's skills as well.

TOP ALL-TIME MANAGER NO. 9: BILL SAMS

An idiosyncratic stock-picking style that favors out-of-favor sectors has been highly successful for Bill Sams, whose two-room office in Dallas consists of one room for his receptionist and another for himself. Though Sams doesn't have a huge staff running around checking figures or an impressive computerized research arsenal, he does have a network of savvy brokers around the country who know him well and know that he'll make a decision on the spot if presented with a good idea for his portfolio. He's owned no technology or health care stocks despite their periods of popularity. He's run the FPA Paramount Fund since 1981, after leaving American Capital Pace where he managed several funds. You're much more likely to find out-of-favor retailers such as Woolworth Corp., unusual financial services firms, energy companies, metals firms, or industrial cyclicals in a Bill Sams portfolio.

This unusual conglomeration of companies prefers decidedly unusual and "un-sexy" stocks. Sams also tends to favor a lot of cash, with his equity exposure seldom over 70 percent in any of the last eight years. Yet the real bottom line is that his conservative portfolio hasn't had a losing year in more than a decade. Even in years in which he trails the overall market, he's usually getting a double-digit return. Meanwhile, in those years in which the market falls apart, such as in 1987, he handily beats the averages. Too bad his eclectic fund with such a terrific long-term record is closed to new investors.

TOP ALL-TIME MANAGER NO. 10: GEORGE VANDERHEIDEN

Like that other Fidelity Investments portfolio manager hero, Peter Lynch, manager George Vanderheiden has an uncanny ability to switch between growth and value philosophies when it can benefit a portfolio. The big difference is that Vanderheiden also employs a macroeconomic overview that analyzes the nation's overall economy. It's used to help decide when in the market cycle the investor should be in cyclical companies, when classic growth companies would be a better choice, and when exactly one should be moving between the two. Lynch, on the other hand, was reported as having said that an investor who spends fifteen minutes a year on macroeconomics wastes ten minutes. Vanderheiden is able to effectively blend his macroeconomic approach with the fundamental bottom-up stock-picking approach that is the trademark of Fidelity managers.

Fidelity Destiny I Fund, which Vanderheiden has run since 1980, has actually been steadier and more consistent than Magellan, although its highs haven't been quite as high. Vanderheiden's flexibility in switching between growth and value has meant that his fund never does poorly in any investment environment. That's why this contractual-plan vehicle, which locks investors into a dollar-cost-averaging investment schedule and doesn't let them out easily for at least a decade, is considered a strong, user-friendly long-term fund. He also manages Fidelity Destiny II and Fidelity Advisor Growth Opportunities. Though of the same generation as Lynch, Vanderheiden has made a remarkable transition from the pen-and-slide-rule genera-tion to the new electronically driven environment of Fidelity's hot young managers. He obviously could find a way to be a winner in any era and in any investment climate.

BEST OF THE REST

Other veteran portfolio managers worthy of note didn't crack the top ten tier but have nonetheless turned in dis-tinguished performances for more than a decade. A list of the best of the rest compiled by Morningstar includes Ralph Wanger of the Acorn Fund; Charles Albers of Guardian Park Avenue; Richard Weiss of Strong Opportunity and Strong Common Stock; Robert Rodriguez of FPA New Income and FPA Capital; Hakan Castegren of Harbor International and Ivy International; Mario Gabelli of the Gabelli Funds; Jerres Gipson of Clipper Fund; William Ruane and Richard Cunniff of Sequoia Fund; Foster Friess of Brandywine; and Stephen Silverman of Merrill Lynch Pacific.

UP AND COMERS

Some portfolio managers have less than a decade of returns under their belt with their current funds, but are already gaining attention with strong, consistent performances. Up-and-coming managers worth close investor scrutiny are Beth Terrana of Fidelity Fund; Daniel Miller of Putnam New Opportunities; John Mussey of Colonial Newport Tiger; Daniel Fuss of Loomis Sayles Bond; John Laporte of T. Rowe Price New Horizons; Carlene Murphy Ziegler of Artisan Small Cap; and Will Danoff of Fidelity Contrafund.

CHAPTER 9

■

PICK AND CHOOSE

"Maybe it does ultimately come down to an educated guess, but I choose my funds only after examining every bit of data, from expense ratios to total returns, from tax consequences to volatility. I like mutual funds because they give average investors like myself some depth to their holdings that no other vehicle can deliver. It's worth a little work, isn't it?"

—LEA ENDLICH, MUTAL FUND
INVESTOR, OVERLAND PARK, KANSAS

Financial planners and investors alike have learned that constructing a comprehensive mutual fund portfolio from today's flood of funds is no easy task. They must research and compare the attributes of all funds under consideration and ponder the personality of the investor.

They must see how the selected funds fit together, in the same manner that Morningstar itself systematically went about putting together its own state-of-the-art 401(k) plan for employees, which has drawn considerable national attention.

Your mission, should you choose to accept it: You're a financial planner with a client who's already invested in the Putnam family of funds. You're helping him add a large-company growth fund, a small-company growth fund, an income stock fund, and an international fund from that same group in order to diversify his holdings.

As he does each and every workday, certified financial planner Michael Lipsey of Creative Financial Group in Atlanta was pecking away on his computer keyboard using the Morningstar OnDisc product to compare various fund portfolios. He also uses the company's Principia program and binder products. "I compare funds versus various indexes and right now I'm looking up volatility in the different Putnam funds," explained Lipsey, in the midst of putting together the fund portfolio. "Most importantly, I examine volatility in one-month periods for my client to see if the funds are compatible with his investment personality."

In his planning practice, mutual funds are the core of a client's assets and Lipsey's primary goal is to obtain predictability of return from funds that have portfolio management continuity. He goes over each fund individually, then uses the computer to compare attributes of different funds, especially what kinds of stocks they hold. He wages a never-ending fight against the trend in which investors simply want each article's list of top funds without fully comprehending the best choices for them. The traditional investment philosophy in using mutual funds is to be more aggressive when you're younger, gradually becoming more conservative as you near retirement so that your principal won't be eroded. However, a lot depends on the personal nature of the investor no matter what his age, and even senior citizens should probably have at least some of their assets in growth investments in order to keep up with the rising cost of living. So you can't simply rely on a formula.

Morningstar is a research tool for planners as they seek the proper fund mix for each client without overlapping portfolios. More than a dozen planners I spoke with said that in the "old" (pre-Morningstar) days, they had little more to go on than total returns of funds. Some of them did their own computer spreadsheets to make unofficial comparisons. Now they have the ability to present explanatory and comparative information to help the client make the final decision on what's best for him. "I've followed Morningstar since its first *Mutual Fund Values* publication and use its products each day to track funds, look for new ones, and present information to clients," related Katharine McGee, a certified financial planner and president of K.A. McGee & Co. in St. Louis. "I've learned that a fund's name doesn't mean much and that changes—such as what managers are on the move—must be followed carefully so that you're not buying last year's performance."

There are no mutual fund investments perfect for anyone and everyone, and there are no shortcuts to the process of building a diversified portfolio, Morningstar asserts. There are no guaranteed approaches to building a suitable mutual fund portfolio either. Furthermore, it's up to the individual to decide whether he's going to get professional advice or go it alone. Going it alone can work well for many investors and, of course, it costs a great deal less than paying for advice. Either way you choose, the results are what count.

"I relied on a broker while I was still working and he never made any money for me, but since retirement I've gotten involved in selecting mutual funds myself and done pretty well," said Carroll Moore, a retired sales and marketing manager who heads the mutual fund study group of the

Kansas City Chapter of the American Association of Individual Investors. "I use Morningstar to make sure I don't duplicate kinds of investments, to find out how consistent a fund is, and to get a more complete listing of the stocks a fund holds."

Morningstar Mutual Funds analysts, in a questionnaire I gave them, were asked how they'd advise an individual investor to go about formulating a winning fund strategy. Their responses urged investors not to procrastinate about implementing their investment plans, but to get started putting money aside on a regular basis immediately; to exhaustively read and study all possible information about funds before making intelligent decisions and then have the confidence to stick with them, or, lacking personal confidence about investing, to hire a quality financial planner for assistance; to carefully define all investment goals and time frames in advance; and to realize that if any mutual fund investment simply seems much too good to be true, there's probably something you're missing.

Morningstar specifically suggests that all investors seeking an appropriate fund mix first ask themselves four basic questions.

QUESTION NO. 1: WHAT ARE MY SPECIFIC INVESTMENT GOALS?

Are you investing with a specific goal in mind—such as financing the purchase of a car or house—or do you have several goals ranging from short-term to long-term? Short-term goals are generally those of three years or less. For example, getting together the down payment for a home purchase could be a short-term goal. Intermediate goals are usually three to ten years, such as the financing of a child's college education. Finally, long-term goals such as planning for retirement are generally ten or more years into the future. Clearly defining your investment objectives based on the time over which you wish to invest should help you devise an effective fund mix.

QUESTION NO. 2:
BASED ON MY GOALS, HOW MUCH RISK CAN I PRUDENTLY ASSUME?

The greater the time you have to invest, the greater amount of risk you're probably willing to tolerate. If an investment goal lies far in the future, you can ride out down periods in an aggressive fund that has potential for high growth. That's because those investments stress capital growth over preservation of initial investment. If your need for the money is sooner rather than later, you're better sticking with more stable investments that emphasize capital preservation. Otherwise, your need for the capital may coincide with a period of depressed fund performance.

QUESTION NO. 3:
BASED ON MY PERSONALITY, HOW MUCH RISK CAN I TOLERATE?

After evaluating your investment goals, it's important not to forget that investing is a highly personal process. You should not select funds purely on the basis of dispassionate, objective criteria. You also need to think about your own personality and how it relates to your investing procedure. For example, if you lie awake nights worrying about the fate of all but the most cautious of investments, your portfolio should probably tend toward more conservative funds. Even if you have a longer investment horizon, you may still personally prefer to venture into stock funds by choosing those that are specifically geared toward cautious investors. This permits you to enjoy some of the long-term growth potential of the equity market with less relative risk.

On the other hand, if you enjoy taking chances, yet your investment goals are short-term, you could allocate a modest percentage of your portfolio to more volatile offerings. This lets you venture into riskier, more exciting areas without betting your entire future on them.

QUESTION NO. 4:
IN CONCLUSION, WHAT SHOULD
MY PORTFOLIO LOOK LIKE?

After identifying the most comfortable investment framework, you can begin to look at the different types of funds offered to see how each might fit into your portfolio. You'll need to decide how many funds to hold. Just remember that there is no optimal number. On the one hand, the more funds into which your assets are divided, the less harm any single fund's losses can inflict. On the other hand, too many funds are difficult to follow conscientiously. If one of your fund choices enjoys a period of outstanding returns, you want to have enough invested in it to make the gains significant. In assessing a fund, consider its place in a broader portfolio. A diversified portfolio is one that offers potential for growth in a variety of market conditions. For example, an international stock fund with fluctuating returns could alone be considered volatile and risky. When added to a portfolio of domestic funds, it could help offset potential declines in the U.S. market.

Any decisions made regarding your portfolio should be reevaluated periodically as the time horizon of your investments changes. For example, retirement investing for a twenty-year-old is long-term and a portfolio can emphasize many aggressive funds. As retirement draws closer, it would be prudent to move into more conservative funds or a guaranteed savings account. Putting short-term dollars into funds that seek primarily to preserve capital will help ensure having money available when you need it, though it does mean sacrificing growth potential.

THE MORNINGSTAR 401(K)

An example of the fund selection process is Morningstar's own 401(k) retirement plan for employees, which was created in 1992. It has been recognized as cutting-edge in selection and range of choices, garning the title of "Rolls-Royce of 401(k) plans" from the *New York Times*. It has a dozen top-flight funds. Average investors can learn a lot about building a long-term investment portfolio from this Morningstar example.

Even though the company has a young workforce with no staffers near retirement age, nine out of ten employees contribute to this 401(k). While only about one-fourth of the money in an average company plan goes into stock funds, more than 95 percent of Morningstar employees have chosen stock funds because they fully recognize the fact that equities offer the greatest growth long-term. "Besides providing for long-term employee well-being and helping to motivate and maintain the workforce, it gives the young people here an opportunity to invest themselves and therefore relate better with the investors they speak with daily," explained Don Phillips, who acknowledges that most workers in their twenties are more concerned with paying their rent than investing long-term. "What's different from so many other 401(k) plans is that we didn't go with just one fund family."

Because it isn't tied to one fund family, the plan offers some excellent portfolio managers with contrasting investment styles and philosophies. The company didn't want to be endorsing any one fund family and didn't think any one company had everything that everyone wanted anyway. For example, giant Fidelity is a titan in most stock fund areas, but its international funds still lag some competing funds. Funds with sales charges were eliminated. An initial list of forty funds was gradually honed down in size through discussions and extensive comparisons. The challenge was finding funds that offered truly distinctive styles and portfolios so that they didn't overlap with one another.

Unlike many other firms' more barebones 401(k) plans, there isn't simply one equity fund choice at Morningstar, but ten different ones that include small-company, growth, value, international, and emerging markets. Phillips, for example, has divided his own money equally among the ten funds because he likes them all and sees considerable differences in their goals and portfolios. In addition, a general bond fund and a money market fund are offered. Morningstar as a rule isn't all that high on those two choices, preferring stocks instead for long-range goals, yet a comprehensive plan should offer conservative choices as well in order to please all employees. The plan made its debut with eight initial funds in 1992, but a subsequent polling of employees found that they wanted a greater number of higher-risk funds. So some worthwhile changes were made in 1994. Two funds in the initial group of offerings had significantly changed and were no longer doing what they'd originally been selected to do. They were replaced with new funds. Several other funds were added as well. Fund strategies always need some ongoing tinkering.

The selection of funds was done through a team approach. First, the employees were asked what funds they'd like to see included. Obviously, employees of Morningstar have considerable information on funds available to them and that definitely helps in this respect. Then Phillips and three other staffers gathered up those choices and figured out which would fit well together into a quality plan. Every two years the funds in the plan are reviewed and it's decided whether there should be changes or additional funds added. Sessions on the 401(k) plan and its offerings are held periodically for the employees. In addition, a number of portfolio managers of the funds stop by Morningstar to speak with analysts, and there's often an opportunity for other staffers to sit in to find out more about how those funds are managed.

The bottom line in Morningstar's experience with the 401(k) plan is that it's important for companies to pay close attention to such plans. Furthermore, you can't simply put something in place and say you've done your job. The real mark of a plan is how well employees use it and how well they understand it. Performance of funds offered must also be monitored closely. As companies move from the traditional defined-benefit retirement plans to these self-directed types of investments, they take on a big responsibility to do additional education about them.

Following is the mix of twelve mutual funds currently included in the Morningstar 401(k) plan and the recent percentage of employee retirement money in each:

Brandywine (17 percent of employee retirement assets), a growth fund whose lead portfolio manager is Foster Friess, has handily beaten the Standard & Poor's 500 over the long haul to rank as a truly elite fund. Brandywine is profiled in Chapter 10, "Twenty-five Time-Tested Funds."

Fidelity Disciplined Equity(15 percent), a growth fund managed by Bradford Lewis, employs computerized artificial intelligence to plot its buying and selling. Prefers large-capitalization stocks and built a reputation as a stellar core holding by not trailing the S&P 500.

PBGH Growth (14 percent), a small-company fund run by Gary Pilgrim, employs an earnings momentum strategy to find the best examples of issues exhibiting earnings growth rates of 20 percent or more. Consistently near the pinnacle of its objective group.

Vanguard International Growth (11 percent), a foreign stock fund managed by Richard Foulkes, emphasizes larger-capitalization stocks. Ranks in the upper level among its peers with an approach that blends value and growth.

Lindner Dividend (11 percent), an income fund managed by Eric Ryback, features a distributed yield from its stock and bond portfolio that consistently tops the group average by 50 to 70 basis points. Has one of the income group's lowest expense ratios and lowest risk ratios.

Fidelity Low-Priced Stock (9 percent), a small-company fund managed by Joel Tillinghast, is enjoined in its prospectus from owning more than 10 percent of any one company. So it must either hold significant cash, spread itself over a huge number of small-caps, or add some larger-cap issues. When taking the latter path in markets favoring large-caps, it has outperformed its peers.

Gabelli Asset (6.5 percent), a growth fund run by Mario Gabelli, tends to hold stocks a very long time because it focuses on long-term value. Buys stocks of companies at the "right price" which should benefit from a possible catalyst that causes the overall market to discover that value.

Montgomery Emerging Markets (6 percent), a diversified fund managed by Josephine Jimenez and Bryan Sudweeks, generates competitive returns with limited risk. Carefully selected portfolio spread fairly evenly across twenty-five to thirty countries and 250 stocks. Half are undervalued blue chips and half undiscovered small-caps.

Vanguard Prime Portfolio Money Market (4 percent), historically one of the highest-yielding money market mutual funds.

T. Rowe Price New Era (2.5 percent), a specialty natural resources fund managed by George Roche, diversifies its exposure by investing in some energy-related industries. It is profiled in Chapter 10 on "Twenty-five Time-Tested Funds."

Selected American Shares (2.5 percent), a growth and income fund managed by Shelby Davis and son Christopher, benefits from the same leadership that made the Davis New York Venture Fund profitable over many years. Its forte is large-capitalization value stocks. Shelby Davis was profiled in Chapter 8, "Legends."

T. Rowe Price New Income (1.5 percent), a high-quality corporate bond fund run by Charles Smith, has benefited from generally accurate interest rate predictions and is less risky than most competitors. Solid, index-like performance makes a fine core holding.

From this list of hits, Morningstar employees pick and choose which grouping of funds meets their individual needs. Because of its own success in the area, it's no surprise Morningstar has identified the growing 401(k) market as one in which it can provide assistance to companies setting up their own programs. It has done so thus far only on a limited basis, but prospects for that portion of the business appear strong.

The strategy used in putting together those funds is exactly what the individual investor must employ in his long-term investing, whether on his own or aided by a financial planner. The trick is to narrow the choices to only good ones, then follow through. Not the easiest task in the world, but hardly an impossible one if you have the necessary information and know how to use it.

CHAPTER 10

■

TWENTY-FIVE
TIME-TESTED FUNDS

"If you have built castles in the air, your work need not be lost; that is where they should be. Now put the foundations under them."
—FROM *Walden*, HENRY DAVID THOREAU

In this modern, hyped world of *fund du jour*, not all mutual funds are here today and forgotten tomorrow. Lists may come and lists may go. Articles may raise consciousness about specific investments and then fade away. Trends will be discussed, economic shifts monitored. But some mutual funds will stand the test of time. They have a long shelf life because they believe fervently in their outstanding strategies and can also roll with the punches.

We now offer the ultimate list of such stalwart long-term funds in major investment objectives, such as growth, value, and income. There are many styles from large-cap,

141

small-cap, fixed-income, and international possibilities. Each of these featured funds can play a unique role in an individual's portfolio because none are exactly alike except in one respect: They're winners, the best the mutual fund industry has to offer. They provide a firm foundation for an entire industry, proof positive that success isn't just a pipe dream but is indeed there for the taking.

This list and narrative on the top twenty-five funds with long-term track records was compiled from extensive interviews with Morningstar staff and careful consideration of significant research information. Years of daily research into the fund industry and those who run its investments went into these choices. The funds' records stand for themselves. These selections are all proven examples with quality track records of more than ten years. All within their various categories are the most "all-weather" examples that can boast excellent management and first-rate consistent returns throughout most of the cycles of the stock market and the economy. Which funds are suitable for you depends, of course, upon your individual goals, risk tolerance, and personal preferences. None will excel each and every year without fail, for the world is a more complex place than that, but it would be difficult to go wrong if you construct a diversified investment foundation for your personal portfolio wisely from this group.

Here then, in alphabetical order, are the cream of the mutual fund crop, the twenty-five best time-tested funds according to Morningstar:

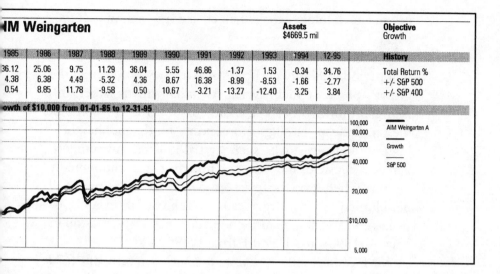

4M Weingarten									**Assets** $4669.5 mil			**Objective** Growth
1985	**1986**	**1987**	**1988**	**1989**	**1990**	**1991**	**1992**	**1993**	**1994**	**12-95**		**History**
36.12	25.06	9.75	11.29	36.04	5.55	46.86	-1.37	1.53	-0.34	34.76		Total Return %
4.38	6.38	4.49	-5.32	4.36	8.67	16.38	-8.99	-8.53	-1.66	-2.77		+/- S&P 500
0.54	8.85	11.78	-9.58	0.50	10.67	-3.21	-13.27	-12.40	3.25	3.84		+/- S&P 400

owth of $10,000 from 01-01-85 to 12-31-95

100,000
80,000 — AIM Weingarten A
60,000 — Growth
40,000 — S&P 500
20,000
$10,000
5,000

1. AIM WEINGARTEN

This large-capitalization growth stock fund never makes a sucker bet on any stock or group. It has fashioned a string of remarkable years by judiciously diversifying its holdings across traditional growth areas. While you'll find its portfolio overweighted in health care, technology, and specialty retailers, you won't see 50 to 60 percent of its assets concentrated in any one of those areas. Don't expect to find many financial, energy, utility, or other value-oriented stocks either. Like most other growth funds, AIM Weingarten suffered disastrous returns from its technology holdings in the second half of 1983 and the first half of 1984, but it rebounded brilliantly, especially in the 1989–91 period. Its large health care stake was subsequently hurt by the political wranglings in Washington, but industrial cyclical and technology stocks helped it forge a strong comeback.

A classic earnings momentum fund, AIM Weingarten will periodically buy cyclical stocks as they go through the growth phase of their cycle. As it has grown larger, this mid-cap fund has become more conservative than some of the smaller-cap earnings-momentum funds and has held bigger-company stocks such as IBM, Texas Instruments, Safeway, PepsiCo, and Pfizer. Though it will undoubtedly be hurt when growth stocks are out of favor, the pain will be blunted by its larger-caps and broad diversity. Co-managers are Jonathan Schoolar (since 1987), Robert Kippes (1993), and David Barnard (1990).

AIM Weingarten's ten-year annualized return of 15.79 percent through the end of 1995 beat the Standard & Poor's 500 by 0.91 of a percentage point, placing it in the upper 9 percent of all growth funds. A $10,000 investment would have grown to $43,308 over the ten-year period. Average risk. Class A shares have a 5.5 percent load. Annual expense ratio is 1.20 percent and 12b-1 fee is 0.30 percent. Minimum initial purchase is $500. Ticker symbol is WEINX. From AIM Capital Management, Houston, 800-347-1919.

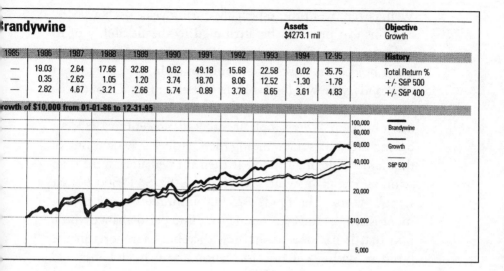

	1985	1986	1987	1988	1989	1990	1991	1992	1993	1994	12-95	History
	—	19.03	2.64	17.66	32.88	0.62	49.18	15.68	22.58	0.02	35.75	Total Return %
	—	0.35	-2.62	1.05	1.20	3.74	18.70	8.06	12.52	-1.30	-1.78	+/- S&P 500
	—	2.82	4.67	-3.21	-2.66	5.74	-0.89	3.78	8.65	3.61	4.83	+/- S&P 400

Brandywine — Assets $4273.1 mil — Objective Growth

Growth of $10,000 from 01-01-86 to 12-31-95

2. BRANDYWINE

If you're a sore loser, you'll love the winning taste of
Brandywine. This high-quality growth fund hasn't had a
down year in the past decade. During this dramatic asset
growth period, it has shifted from a small-cap to a mid-cap
orientation. It now bears a great deal of similarity to AIM
Weingarten, with holdings such as IBM and Texas
Instruments in its portfolio. Scott Paper, Amgen, and
Household International have been among other investment components. The major difference between the two
funds is that Brandywine is much more willing to concentrate its assets in a market sector where it sees the best
opportunities. For example, for much of 1995 it had a dar-
ing 70 percent of its assets in volatile technology stocks.
Brandywine has actually tended to be stronger than AIM

Weingarten over time, especially during years such as 1992, and this can probably be attributed to the flexibility of its style. Lead portfolio manager Foster Friess (since 1985) often holds a tremendous amount of cash.

Brandywine will be a volatile investment on a month-to-month basis. You should therefore have a long-term investment horizon. For example, it rose 2.64 percent in 1987, but during the weeks surrounding the October crash was one of the hardest-hit of all funds. It then immediately went on a winning streak in which it whipped the S&P 500 for six straight years. The fund's $25,000 minimum initial investment is steep. However, besides the fine performance, you'll find that it has one of the best shareholder reports in the business, with a raft of information about its holdings and philosophy. Anyone who reads it will have an excellent sense of what the fund does. The economies of scale derived from having a smaller number of accounts makes possible its outstanding support materials, such as a first-rate quarterly letter. This fund is held in Morningstar's own 401(k) plan for employees.

Brandywine's ten-year annualized return of 18.63 percent through the end of 1995 beat that of the S&P 500 by 3.75 percentage points, ranking it in the upper 3 percent of growth funds. A $10,000 investment would have grown to $55,196 over the ten-year period. Above-average risk. It is a no-load fund. Annual expense ratio is 1.07 percent. Minimum initial purchase is $25,000 (for IRA as well). Ticker symbol is BRWIX. From Brandywine Fund, Greenville, Delaware, 800-656-3017.

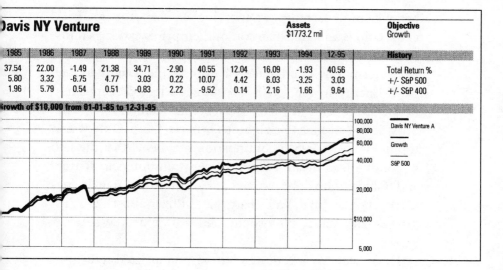

	1985	1986	1987	1988	1989	1990	1991	1992	1993	1994	12-95	History
	37.54	22.00	-1.49	21.38	34.71	-2.90	40.55	12.04	16.09	-1.93	40.56	Total Return %
	5.80	3.32	-6.75	4.77	3.03	0.22	10.07	4.42	6.03	-3.25	3.03	+/- S&P 500
	1.96	5.79	0.54	0.51	-0.83	2.22	-9.52	0.14	2.16	1.66	9.64	+/- S&P 400

Davis NY Venture — Assets $1773.2 mil — Objective Growth

Growth of $10,000 from 01-01-85 to 12-31-95

Davis NY Venture A / Growth / S&P 500

3. DAVIS NEW YORK VENTURE

If you could own just one stock mutual fund, this would be a spectacular choice. A terrific "avoider of disaster," Davis New York Venture has been a steady, competitive fund for an extended period of time. It often winds up in the upper 20 to 35 percent of growth funds in performance, and has beaten the overall market in nine of the past eleven years. Some portfolio managers can outstrip the market several years running, but they often eventually get hammered. Smooth-sailing Shelby Davis, profiled in the chapter on portfolio manager legends, makes certain there aren't many peaks and valleys for his investors along the way. His conservative style seeks out low-cost issues and he's always willing to change with the times as trends evolve.

Shelby (since 1969) and son Christopher (since 1995), the fund's co–portfolio manager, discover stocks likely to benefit from earnings growth higher than the market's expectations and an expansion of their price/earnings multiple when the market does finally recognize that growth. They term this confluence of events "the Davis double play." Energy in the 1970s, consumer-oriented companies in the 1980s, and financial services and technology in the early 1990s all met this rigorous criteria. Coca-Cola was a top holding in 1995, a continuation of a belief that the fall of communism meant billions of new consumers in Russia and China who'd be attracted by consumer staples. Yet stocks such as Intel, Wells Fargo, and Pfizer also fit into its growth-and-value philosophy at that time. Whatever works!

Davis New York Venture's ten-year annualized return of 17 percent through the end of 1995 beat the S&P 500 by 2.12 percentage points, ranking it in the upper 7 percent of growth funds. A $10,000 investment would have grown to $48,090 over the ten-year period. Average risk. Class A shares have a 4.75 percent load. Annual expense ratio is 0.90 percent and 12b-1 fee is 0.25 percent. Minimum initial purchase is $1,000, or $250 for IRAs. Ticker symbol is NYVTX. From Davis Selected Advisers, Santa Fe, New Mexico, 800-279-0279.

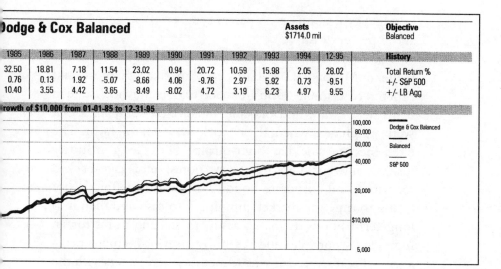

)odge & Cox Balanced											Assets $1714.0 mil	Objective Balanced
1985	1986	1987	1988	1989	1990	1991	1992	1993	1994	12-95		History
32.50	18.81	7.18	11.54	23.02	0.94	20.72	10.59	15.98	2.05	28.02		Total Return %
0.76	0.13	1.92	-5.07	-8.66	4.06	-9.76	2.97	5.92	0.73	-9.51		+/- S&P 500
10.40	3.55	4.42	3.65	8.49	-8.02	4.72	3.19	6.23	4.97	9.55		+/- LB Agg

Growth of $10,000 from 01-01-85 to 12-31-95

Dodge & Cox Balanced
Balanced
S&P 500

4. DODGE & COX BALANCED

The Dodge & Cox Group makes it all look so easy. It really
doesn't seem to care much about being in the mutual fund
industry, emphasizing instead its main business of doing
money management for high-net-worth individuals. It has
outstanding funds with excellent track records, yet shies
away from all forms of publicity and doesn't bother to
advertise its triumphs. Whenever a screen of top-performing
long-term funds is run by computer, the Dodge & Cox
name comes up time and time again. Many of today's portfolio managers talk about having a long-term time horizon,
but their active trading indicates they aren't all that serious
about it. Dodge & Cox Balanced, however, has portfolio
turnover of 10 to 20 percent each year, which means it really
does have a serious time horizon of five to ten years. It is a
conservative, classic balanced fund holding both stocks and

149

bonds. A typical mix is 55 percent stocks, 40 percent bonds, and 5 percent cash.

The equity side emphasizes blue-chip companies such as General Motors, IBM, Citicorp, American Express, and Procter & Gamble. Don't expect to see the hottest tech firms here. You'll find old-line, established companies that were purchased when their stock was out of favor. The fixed-income side has high-quality, fairly long maturity instruments, including Treasury notes, mortgage-backed securities, and corporate bonds. This fund is definitely not trying to time the market, jumping into cash and then into long-term bonds. It makes a superb starting point for an individual's portfolio and is run by a seven-member management team, three of whose members have been with the fund for more than fifteen years.

Dodge & Cox Balanced's ten-year annualized return of 13.56 percent through the end of 1995 was 1.32 percentage points below the S&P 500. That ranked in the fifth percentile of balanced funds. A $10,000 investment would have grown to $35,683 over the ten-year period. Below-average risk. It is a no-load fund. Annual expense ratio is 0.58 percent. Minimum initial purchase is $2,500, or $1,000 for IRAs. Ticker symbol is DODBX. From Dodge & Cox Group, San Francisco, 800-621-3979.

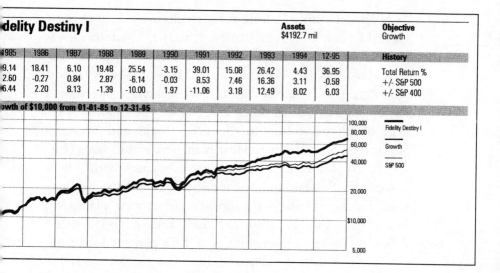

delity Destiny I											Assets $4192.7 mil	Objective Growth
1985	1986	1987	1988	1989	1990	1991	1992	1993	1994	12-95		History
9.14	18.41	6.10	19.48	25.54	-3.15	39.01	15.08	26.42	4.43	36.95		Total Return %
2.60	-0.27	0.84	2.87	-6.14	-0.03	8.53	7.46	16.36	3.11	-0.58		+/- S&P 500
6.44	2.20	8.13	-1.39	-10.00	1.97	-11.06	3.18	12.49	8.02	6.03		+/- S&P 400

5. FIDELITY DESTINY I

This long-distance performer isn't for everyone, since it's one of the last of the old contractual-plan vehicles, locking investors into a dollar-cost-averaging investment schedule and making it tough to get out for at least ten years. If you take your money out after three years, you stand to be charged as much as 27 percent for Fidelity's services. However, the primary negative against such plans is that you can't be confident about management for that long a time period, and that definitely isn't the case with Fidelity Destiny I. Since taking over the fund in 1980, portfolio manager George Vanderheiden has had only two below-average calendar years on his record versus the overall growth group. Impressively, for those two years, 1985 and 1989, he still had gains of 29 percent and 25 percent respectively.

Fidelity Destiny I's long-term results are nearly unbeaten and its risk scores are relatively modest. Vanderheiden is profiled in the chapter on portfolio manager legends. His style isn't all that different from that of Shelby Davis, although he's less interested in market themes and more a student of macroeconomics. In 1995 he put about 20 percent of his portfolio into financial stocks and a similar amount into technology. Most managers would have chosen to emphasize one or the other, but not both. He is completely flexibile in his stock choices. Vanderheiden also runs Fidelity Destiny II, another contractual plan with lower fees and similarly excellent results, and Fidelity Advisor Growth Opportunities, a 4.75 percent load fund with no contractual obligation. Both are growth funds.

Fidelity Destiny I's ten-year annualized return of 18.10 percent through the end of 1995 beat the S&P 500 by 3.22 percentage points. It ranked in the fourth percentile of all growth funds. A $10,000 investment would have grown to $52,805 over the ten years. Below-average risk. There's an 8.24 percent load. Annual expense ratio is 0.68 percent. Minimum initial purchase is $50 under ongoing contribution agreement. Ticker symbol is FDESX. From Fidelity Group, Boston, 800-752-2347.

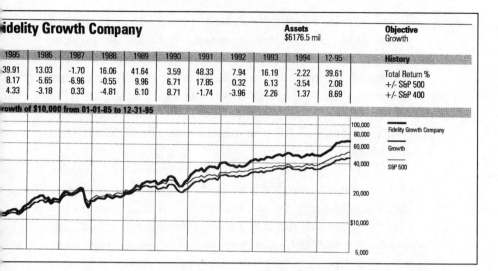

idelity Growth Company										**Assets** $6176.5 mil		**Objective** Growth
1985	1986	1987	1988	1989	1990	1991	1992	1993	1994	12-95		**History**
39.91	13.03	-1.70	16.06	41.64	3.59	48.33	7.94	16.19	-2.22	39.61		Total Return %
8.17	-5.65	-6.96	-0.55	9.96	6.71	17.85	0.32	6.13	-3.54	2.08		+/- S&P 500
4.33	-3.18	0.33	-4.81	6.10	8.71	-1.74	-3.96	2.26	1.37	8.69		+/- S&P 400

Growth of $10,000 from 01-01-85 to 12-31-95

100,000 / 80,000 — Fidelity Growth Company
60,000 — Growth
40,000 — S&P 500
20,000
$10,000
5,000

6. FIDELITY GROWTH COMPANY

Fidelilty's Young Turks are now mature managers with a decade of experience under their belts. A large number of young managers were hired in the 1980s. After traning under the sainted Peter Lynch, portfolio manager Robert Stansky took over this lackluster-performing fund's few assets in 1987 and did a dynamic job with it. Long-term results have been strong. Fidelity Growth Company became more large-cap in orientation under Stansky. It may shift back a bit toward smaller-cap stocks under new manager Lawrence Greenberg (since 1996), who has favored them in his role as manager of Fidelity Emerging Growth. Yet Stansky's imprint still remains on this fund.

The stock-picking screen employed here goes beyond earnings growth rates to consider depth and sustainability of growth, as indicated by sales revenues and unit volume.

These serve as effective indicators. For example, he picked up on slowing unit sales in consumer staples and got out before that sector subsequently blew up. Volatility has been contained by investing in quality companies and getting out at the right time, in much the same way that AIM Weingarten and Brandywine do. Stansky tends to use more cash than other Fidelity managers, typically totaling 10 to 15 percent of assets.

Fidelity Growth Company's ten-year annualized return of 17 percent through the end of 1995 beat the S&P 500 by 2.12 percentage points, which ranked it in the upper 8 percent of growth funds. A $10,000 investment would have grown to $48,059 over ten years. Above-average risk. There's a 3 percent load. Annual expense ratio is 0.95 percent. Ticker symbol is FDGRX. Minimum initial investment is $2,500, or $500 for an IRA. From Fidelity Group, Boston, 800-544-8888.

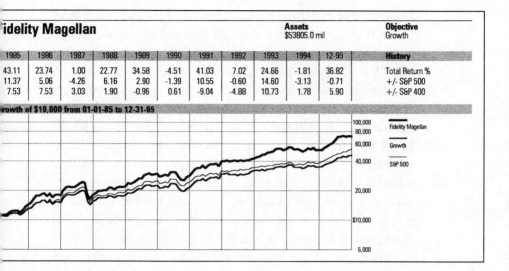

idelity Magellan									Assets $53805.0 mil		Objective Growth	
1985	1986	1987	1988	1989	1990	1991	1992	1993	1994	12-95	History	
43.11	23.74	1.00	22.77	34.58	-4.51	41.03	7.02	24.66	-1.81	36.82	Total Return %	
11.37	5.06	-4.26	6.16	2.90	-1.39	10.55	-0.60	14.60	-3.13	-0.71	+/- S&P 500	
7.53	7.53	3.03	1.90	-0.96	0.61	-9.04	-4.88	10.73	1.78	5.90	+/- S&P 400	

Growth of $10,000 from 01-01-85 to 12-31-95

7. FIDELITY MAGELLAN

Large bodies of money can be managed effectively and great organizations run great funds. That's the lesson of giant Fidelity Magellan, as Morningstar has consistently pointed out over the years. Getting bigger doesn't have to turn a portfolio into an index-like fund. Peter Lynch in the 1980s was flexible, willing to take big positions in bonds or Chrysler when it was teetering on the brink of bankruptcy. His successor, Morris Smith, built a portfolio of highly stable companies. When Smith left, Jeff Vinik repositioned it in natural resources and technology, before making a shift to financial services. Latest manager Robert Stansky has more of a large-capitalization growth-stock background. When running Fidelity Growth Company, Stansky invested primarily in blue chips and technology. Magellan has been a winner mostly because it isn't wedded to one market sector or one investment approach. It is built on a basic belief that turning over enough rocks, looking at enough opportunities, reading enough annual reports, and examining what is special in each stock's case will get the job done.

Magellan in its current form offers a slim chance of winding up in the top 10 percent of funds over the next decade. But, as pointed out in Chapter 4, the strong likelihood of ranking consistently in the upper one-third is nothing to sniff at. No, it won't make money in a year when stocks don't make money, for it doesn't possess some sort of miraculous ability to beat the market no matter what. However, it has done well in a variety of different markets and it therefore is a fund that investors have come to depend upon as a long-term holding. What's not to like?

Fidelity Magellan's ten-year average annualized return of 17.42 percent through 1995 beat the S&P 500 by 2.54 percentage points. It ranked in the upper 6 percent of growth funds for that period. A $10,000 investment would have grown to $49,820 during that ten-year time frame. Average risk. It has a 3 percent load. Annual expense ratio is 0.96 percent. Ticker symbol is FMAGX. Minimum initial investment is $2,500, or $500 in IRAs. From Fidelity Group, Boston, 800-544-8888.

Fidelity Puritan

												Assets $15158.3 mil	Objective Balanced

1985	1986	1987	1988	1989	1990	1991	1992	1993	1994	12-95	History
28.71	20.75	-1.79	18.89	19.60	-6.35	24.46	15.43	21.45	1.78	21.46	Total Return %
-3.03	2.07	-7.05	2.28	-12.08	-3.23	-6.02	7.81	11.39	0.46	-16.07	+/- S&P 500
6.61	5.49	-4.55	11.00	5.07	-15.31	8.46	8.03	11.70	4.70	2.99	+/- LB Agg

Growth of $10,000 from 01-01-85 to 12-31-95

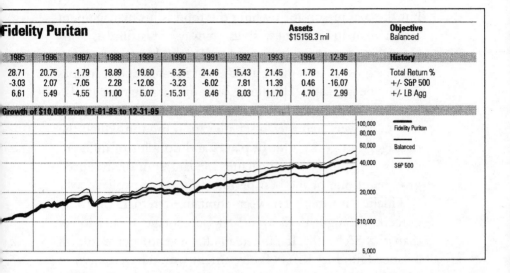

8. FIDELITY PURITAN

A flexibly managed balanced fund over the years, Puritan owned a lot of junk bonds in the late 1980s that hurt it in 1990. Today, however, it sticks mostly with conservative, higher-quality bonds. But while its stocks tend to be large-cap, the fund isn't as conservative as, say, Dodge & Cox Balanced. There is definite flexibility involved in its management. Portfolio manager Richard Fentin (since 1987) will sometimes hold nearly 70 percent of the portfolio in stocks, which is unusual for a balanced fund. He also has more than one-fourth of equity holdings in foreign markets. As a result of its value investment outlook and contrarian streak, Puritan tends to perform more like Fidelity's income offerings, Fidelity Equity-Income I and II, than traditional balanced funds.

Fentin has a reputation for not talking much publicly,

but the real reason for owning the fund is his management rather than his interview skills anyway. This fund is considered particularly attractive for IRAs when the investor wants exposure to numerous different markets and securities all in one package. The fund's income orientation is also another reason why it fits well into that setting. It's much like an actively managed asset allocation fund in which the manager can go to a lot of places and do a lot of different things. A popular fund, Puritan is the largest of the balanced group and one of the best performing in it as well.

Fidelity Puritan's ten-year annualized return of 13.04 percent through 1995 was 1.84 percentage points lower than the S&P 500. It ranked in the seventh percentile of balanced funds. A $10,000 investment would have grown to $34,051 during that period. Average risk. It has a 2 percent load. Annual expense ratio is 0.77 percent. Ticker symbol is FPURX. Minimum initial investment is $2,500, or $500 for IRAs. From Fidelity Group, Boston, 800-544-8888.

FPA New Income											Assets $226.5 mil	Objective Corp Bond--General

1985	1986	1987	1988	1989	1990	1991	1992	1993	1994	12-95	History
21.31	11.11	7.87	8.55	12.23	8.38	18.80	11.12	10.17	1.46	14.36	Total Return %
-0.79	-4.15	5.11	0.66	-2.30	-0.58	2.80	3.72	0.42	4.38	-4.11	+/- LB Agg
-2.75	-5.42	5.31	-0.67	-1.75	1.23	0.29	2.42	-2.00	5.38	-7.88	+/- LB Corp

Growth of $10,000 from 01-01-85 to 12-31-95

FPA New Income

Corp Bond--General

LB Aggregate

9. FPA NEW INCOME

This relatively small bond fund has a decidedly conservative base, but has displayed innovation by adding to its portfolio foreign bonds from places such as Israel and Turkey, as well as Ginnie Mae mobile home bonds. You don't see either of those in most bond portfolios. Furthermore, portfolio manager Robert Rodriguez (since 1984) has been a terrific predictor of interest rate movements, moving aggressively on the durations of his holdings and capable of making money even in years when interest rates spike upward. It has performed well in many different types of environments over the years. Rodriguez has a contrarian mind-set, loading up on convertibles after their late-1980s slide, and buying high-yield bonds after their 1990 collapse. Both moves paid off.

The fund must invest at least 75 percent of assets in U.S.

government securities, nonconvertible debt securities rated at least AA, U.S. dollar–denominated Canadian government debt, repurchase agreements, and cash. The balance of assets may be invested in securities rated below AA and/or convertible securities. A drawback to the fund's growth has been its 4.50 percent load, since most investors don't like the idea of paying a significant load on a bond fund. Interestingly, Rodriguez also manages FPA Capital, a successful stock fund. It's unusual to see a manager capably run both stock and bond funds at the same time.

FPA New Income's ten-year annualized return of 10.32 percent through 1995 beat the Lehman Brothers Index aggregate by 0.69 of a percentage point. That ranked it in the upper 10 percent of general bond funds. A $10,000 investment would have grown to $26,716 over the ten years. Below-average risk. There's a 4.50 percent load and 0.68 percent annual expense ratio. Ticker symbol is FPNIX. Minimum initial purchase is $1,500, or $100 for IRAs. From FPA Funds, Los Angeles, 800-982-4372.

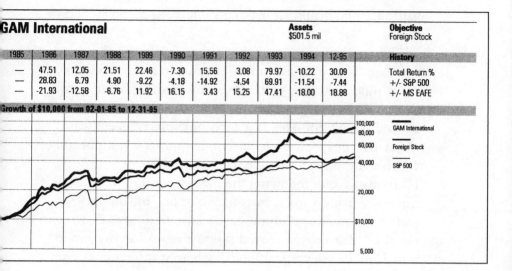

GAM International   Assets $501.5 mil   Objective Foreign Stock

1985	1986	1987	1988	1989	1990	1991	1992	1993	1994	12-95	History
—	47.51	12.05	21.51	22.46	-7.30	15.56	3.08	79.97	-10.22	30.09	Total Return %
—	28.83	6.79	4.90	-9.22	-4.18	-14.92	-4.54	69.91	-11.54	-7.44	+/- S&P 500
—	-21.93	-12.58	-6.76	11.92	16.15	3.43	15.25	47.41	-18.00	18.88	+/- MS EAFE

Growth of $10,000 from 02-01-85 to 12-31-95

10. GAM INTERNATIONAL

This is a truly amazing international fund, ranking number one in its group since its inception in 1985. A product of London-based Global Asset Management, it's also one of the most innovative funds. Portfolio manager John Horseman (since 1990) pays no attention at all to typical country weightings. For a while, he didn't care if he owned any Japanese holdings at all, and at one point had 20 percent of his portfolio in New Zealand equities. The fund therefore doesn't perform like the typical international benchmarks, but bravely carves out its own path. It does, however, occasionally have the potential to embarrass itself. For example, it stumbled badly with a 10.22 percent loss in 1994, a year in which the typical international fund's return was flat. Horseman more than made up for it with a 30.09 percent gain in 1995, thanks to making some bold currency decisions.

This is a bet on the manager, rather than going the route of many international funds that operate virtually like index funds. It's more speculative and doesn't guarantee you that you'll be going wherever the international markets are headed. Don't consider it a core holding. It recently had about half of its portfolio in bonds, and its stock portion was heavily into the utility, services, and financial groups. Horseman avoids following the masses, but uses macroeconomic evaluation and sector analysis to find off-the-beaten-path investment opportunities. Because of the fund's composition, Morningstar moved it into a new objective group called "multi-asset global funds," where it still ranks as one of the best.

GAM International's ten-year annualized return of 19.03 percent through 1995 beat the S&P 500 by 4.15 percentage points to rank in the first percentile of foreign funds. A $10,000 investment would have grown to $57,050 during that ten-year period. Average risk. There's a 5 percent load and 1.60 percent annual expense ratio. Ticker symbol is GAMNX. Minimum initial purchase is $10,000, or $2,000 for IRAs. From GAM International Management, New York, 800-426-4685.

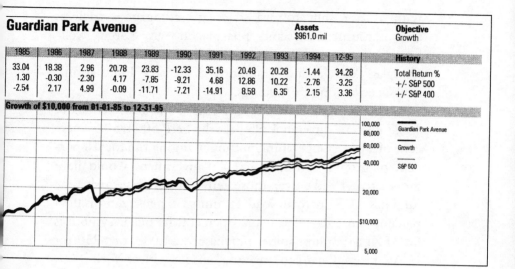

Guardian Park Avenue											Assets $961.0 mil	Objective Growth
1985	1986	1987	1988	1989	1990	1991	1992	1993	1994	12-95		**History**
33.04	18.38	2.96	20.78	23.83	-12.33	35.16	20.48	20.28	-1.44	34.28		Total Return %
1.30	-0.30	-2.30	4.17	-7.85	-9.21	4.68	12.86	10.22	-2.76	-3.25		+/- S&P 500
-2.54	2.17	4.99	-0.09	-11.71	-7.21	-14.91	8.58	6.35	2.15	3.36		+/- S&P 400

Growth of $10,000 from 01-01-85 to 12-31-95

100,000
80,000 — Guardian Park Avenue
60,000
Growth
40,000
S&P 500
20,000
$10,000
5,000

11. GUARDIAN PARK AVENUE

A pioneer in quantitative screens that include a stock-scoring system on valuation and momentum, Guardian Park Avenue relies on the ability of its proven portfolio manager to interpret all of them correctly. Changing market conditions can therefore change the positioning of this growth fund significantly, unlike many core funds that stick closely with a basic style through thick and thin. For example, portfolio manager Charles Albers (since 1972) began in 1993 to move the fund from a small-cap value to a large-cap blend.

His various movements over the years, with the glaring exception of 1990 when the fund fell 12.33 percent, have been quite masterful. That's fitting for someone who was one of the first to espouse the combined concept of value and growth years ago. Technology, industrial cyclicals, and financials were among portfolio holdings in the early 1990s, with a later shift toward stable growth groups such as telecommunications and pharmaceuticals. Large, well-known companies such as IBM, Exxon, McDonnell Douglas, Merck, and Computer Associates International have been among its holdings.

Guardian Park Avenue's ten-year annualized return of 15.27 percent through 1995 beat the S&P 500 by 0.39 percent of a percentage point, putting it among the top 16 percent of growth funds. A $10,000 investment would have grown to $41,431 over those ten years. Average risk. The fund has a 4.50 percent load. Its annual expense ratio is 0.84 percent and 12b-1 fee is 0.25 percent. Its ticker symbol is GPAFX. Minimum initial purchase is $1,000, or $250 for IRAs. From Guardian Investor Services, New York, 800-221-3253.

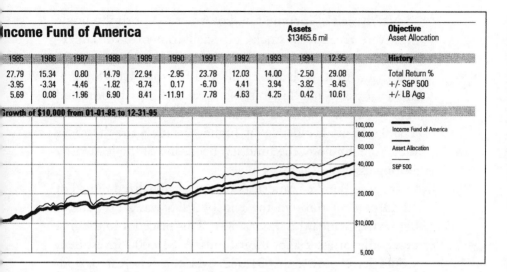

Income Fund of America

Assets
$13465.6 mil

Objective
Asset Allocation

	1985	1986	1987	1988	1989	1990	1991	1992	1993	1994	12-95	History
	27.79	15.34	0.80	14.79	22.94	-2.95	23.78	12.03	14.00	-2.50	29.08	Total Return %
	-3.95	-3.34	-4.46	-1.82	-8.74	0.17	-6.70	4.41	3.94	-3.82	-8.45	+/- S&P 500
	5.69	0.08	-1.96	6.90	8.41	-11.91	7.78	4.63	4.25	0.42	10.61	+/- LB Agg

Growth of $10,000 from 01-01-85 to 12-31-95

Income Fund of America

Asset Allocation

S&P 500

12. INCOME FUND OF AMERICA

This asset allocation fund is even more conservative than
Dodge & Cox Balanced. Its target is the investor who prizes
income over total return, but doesn't want to ignore return
altogether and doesn't want to go the traditional route of
buying bonds, living off the coupons, and not seeing principal grow. It's run by a team of six managers, each of which
receives sole responsibility for running a specific portion of
the portfolio's assets. Abner Goldstine (since 1973), George
Miller (1976), and Richard Schotte (1978) are the most
senior members of the team. The fund recently had nearly
40 percent of its portfolio in bonds that ranged all the way
from higher-quality government issues to junk bonds. It has
admittedly had the advantage over the past decade of a period of declining rates, yet it's obvious that this team knows
how to string together different ways of collecting income.

Nearly half of Income Fund of America's portfolio holdings were recently in stocks, especially out-of-favor larger-caps. For example, it has had significant holdings in pharmaceuticals such as Eli Lilly and Bristol-Myers Squibb, financial stocks like Lincoln National and First Union, and energy stocks such as Phillips Petroleum and Texaco. Thanks to its avoidance of higher-octane growth stocks such as technology, the fund has been one of the least risky among asset-allocation vehicles.

Income Fund of America's ten-year annualized return of 12.22 percent through the end of 1995 was 2.66 percent below the Standard & Poor's 500. This placed it in the first percentile of asset allocation funds. A $10,000 investment would have grown to $31,672 over the ten-year period. Below-average risk. It has a 5.75 percent load. Annual expense ratio is 0.65 percent and 12b-1 fee is 0.25 percent. Ticker symbol is AMECX. Minimum initial purchase is $1,000, or $250 for an IRA. From American Funds, San Francisco, 800-421-4120.

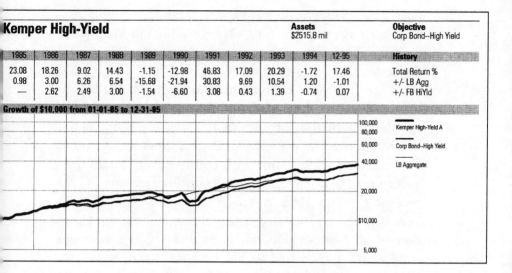

Kemper High-Yield									Assets $2515.8 mil			Objective Corp Bond--High Yield		
1985	1986	1987	1988	1989	1990	1991	1992	1993	1994	12-95		History		
23.08	18.26	9.02	14.43	-1.15	-12.98	46.83	17.09	20.29	-1.72	17.46		Total Return %		
0.98	3.00	6.26	6.54	-15.68	-21.94	30.83	9.69	10.54	1.20	-1.01		+/- LB Agg		
—	2.62	2.49	3.00	-1.54	-6.60	3.08	0.43	1.39	-0.74	0.07		+/- FB HiYld		

Growth of $10,000 from 01-01-85 to 12-31-95

- Kemper High-Yield A
- Corp Bond--High Yield
- LB Aggregate

13. KEMPER HIGH-YIELD

While the same cannot be said for all of the company's investment products, Kemper High-Yield has certainly done its family proud. Over the past fifteen years, Kemper's deep credit research department has helped the fund out-perform the typical high-yield fund thirteen times. Its double-digit long-term returns look great to investors and have been accomplished by taking on only average risk. It did spectacularly well in the 1980s and its performance in the 1990s has featured a 46.83 percent gain in 1991. Co-portfolio managers Michael McNamara (since 1990) and Harry Resis Jr. (1992) know when to hold 'em and know when to fold 'em. It has prospered in less-stable deferred-interest and payment-in-kind bonds when they believe the issuing companies' prospects are sound.

Because the fund is so large, it's also able to make its

voice heard when it buys into junk issues, demanding features such as call protection. Over time, a high-yield bond fund won't provide stock-market-like returns, but should do better than regular bond returns. While a high-yield bond is still a bond, it should really be considered a hybrid because it's weaker in credit and therefore tends to fluctuate along with the fortunes of the business more like a stock. Kemper High-Yield would be a good second bond fund, after investing in one with higher-quality bonds first.

Kemper High-Yield's ten-year annualized return of 11.72 percent through 1995 was 2.23 percent better than the Lehman Brothers Index aggregate, placing it in the top 1 percent of all high-yield bond funds. A $10,000 investment would have grown to $30,304 over the ten-year period. Below-average risk. It has a 4.50 percent load. Annual expense ratio is 0.90 percent. Ticker symbol is KHYAX. Minimum initial purchase is $1,000, or $250 for an IRA. From Kemper Financial Services, Chicago, 800-621-1048.

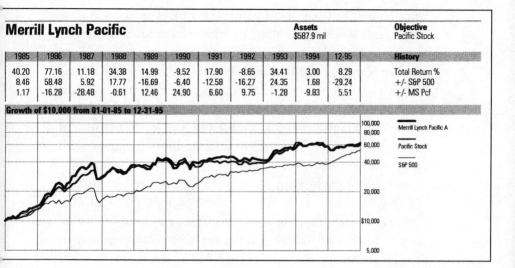

Merrill Lynch Pacific

Assets $587.9 mil

Objective Pacific Stock

	1985	1986	1987	1988	1989	1990	1991	1992	1993	1994	12-95	History
	40.20	77.16	11.18	34.38	14.99	-9.52	17.90	-8.65	34.41	3.00	8.29	Total Return %
	8.46	58.48	5.92	17.77	-16.69	-6.40	-12.58	-16.27	24.35	1.68	-29.24	+/- S&P 500
	1.17	-16.28	-28.48	-0.61	12.46	24.90	6.60	9.75	-1.28	-9.83	5.51	+/- MS Pcf

Growth of $10,000 from 01-01-85 to 12-31-95

Merrill Lynch Pacific A

Pacific Stock

S&P 500

14. MERRILL LYNCH PACIFIC

Brokerage house funds don't have to be dull and predictable. Just look at Merrill Lynch Pacific, which has without a doubt been the best-run Pacific Basin fund in existence. It doesn't operate as an index-like fund, and therefore is sometimes at odds with the general logic in the region. The fund did exceptionally well in the 1980s when the Japanese market was on a roll, turning in a 40.20 percent performance in 1985. It's also held its own in the 1990s, with a 34.41 percent gain in 1993. Best of all, portfolio manager Stephen Silverman (since 1983) has done an excellent job of keeping U.S. investor holdings flat in difficult times when the Pacific markets are in complete collapse. Unlike the funds of many other managers, Silverman's didn't get killed when the Japanese investment bubble burst.

Merrill Lynch Pacific owns many big Japanese conglomerates, but has also begun some plays in the Chinese market. It has been willing to take enormous positions in individual stocks such as Murata Manufacturing, Toyo Seikan Kaisha, and Mitsubishi Heavy Industries. The Pacific Basin is a speculative and specialized market play, but this still relatively small fund offers a way to get involved in a fairly conservative fashion. Guided by the longest tenure in its objective class, this fund has a stable list of holdings with low turnover rates.

Merrill Lynch Pacific's ten-year annualized return of 16.09 percent through 1995 beat the S&P 500 by 1.21 percentage points, ranking it in the first percentile of Pacific stock funds. A $10,000 investment would have grown to $44,469 over the ten-year period. Above-average risk. It has a 5.25 percent load. Annual expense ratio is 0.91 percent. Ticker symbol is MAPCX. Minimum initial purchase is $1,000, or $100 for an IRA. From Merrill Lynch Asset Management, New York, 800-637-3863.

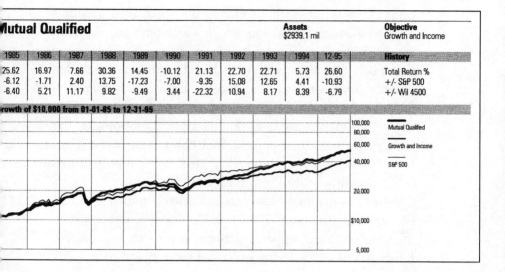

Mutual Qualified											**Assets** $2939.1 mil	**Objective** Growth and Income
1985	**1986**	**1987**	**1988**	**1989**	**1990**	**1991**	**1992**	**1993**	**1994**	**12-95**	**History**
25.62	16.97	7.66	30.36	14.45	-10.12	21.13	22.70	22.71	5.73	26.60	Total Return %
-6.12	-1.71	2.40	13.75	-17.23	-7.00	-9.35	15.08	12.65	4.41	-10.93	+/- S&P 500
-6.40	5.21	11.17	9.82	-9.49	3.44	-22.32	10.94	8.17	8.39	-6.79	+/- Wil 4500

Growth of $10,000 from 01-01-85 to 12-31-95

Mutual Qualified

Growth and Income

S&P 500

15. MUTUAL QUALIFIED

Being an extremist isn't always considered a positive, but Mutual Qualified's extreme value strategy, which seeks out turnaround and bankruptcy situations, has been positive for its investors. If a company has a good franchise or niche position but has fallen completely out of favor with the market, portfolio manager Michael Price (since 1980) is interested. Sears, Roebuck was a good example of that. He's also an activist, sometimes buying large stakes in a company's voting shares to be able to push management to enhance shareholder value. In early 1995 he announced that he had a 6.1 percent stake in Chase Manhattan and successfully agitated for it to merge with Chemical Bank in the third quarter. Price is profiled in the chapter on portfolio manager legends.

Mutual Qualified was originally to be run differently

171

from other funds, with an emphasis on qualified accounts such as IRAs or Keoghs in which short-term capital gains wouldn't be felt. However, in light of changes in the tax law that made this less necessary, it hasn't been run much differently from some of Price's other funds. It did wonderfully in the mid- to late 1980s and relatively poorly in 1989–91 when growth stock investing was booming. For example, it fell 10.12 percent in 1990. If you invest long-term, you'll be fine. But realize that there will be times when you'll be out of step with the market.

Mutual Qualified's ten-year annualized return of 15.21 percent beat the S&P 500 by 0.33 of a percentage point. That put it in the upper 5 percent of growth and income funds. A $10,000 investment would have grown to $41,207 over that ten-year period. Low risk. It is a no-load fund. Annual expense ratio is 0.73 percent. Ticker symbol is MQIFX. Minimum initial purchase is $1,000. From Heine Securities, Short Hills, New Jersey, 800-553-3014.

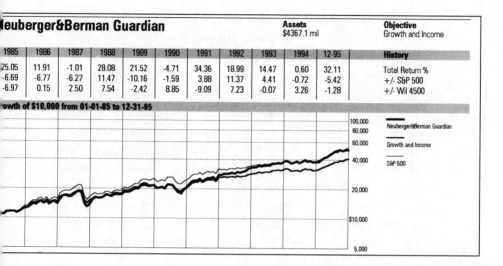

Neuberger&Berman Guardian											Assets $4367.1 mil	Objective Growth and Income
1985	1986	1987	1988	1989	1990	1991	1992	1993	1994	12-95		History
25.05	11.91	-1.01	28.08	21.52	-4.71	34.36	18.99	14.47	0.60	32.11		Total Return %
-6.69	-6.77	-6.27	11.47	-10.16	-1.59	3.88	11.37	4.41	-0.72	-5.42		+/- S&P 500
-6.97	0.15	2.50	7.54	-2.42	8.85	-9.09	7.23	-0.07	3.26	-1.28		+/- Wil 4500

Growth of $10,000 from 01-01-85 to 12-31-95

16. NEUBERGER & BERMAN GUARDIAN

Unlike Michael Price's Mutual Qualified, Neuberger & Berman Guardian goes after high-quality value stocks. It picked up some health care companies several years ago when that group started weakening and also bought some technology stocks when they were in trouble. It has owned Micron Technology, certainly an unusual value stock purchase, and well-known financial holdings like Citicorp. Other stocks have included AT&T, Chrysler, and Capital Cities/ABC. Many of the fund's choices wouldn't make it through the screens of other value managers because they aren't dirt cheap. Guardian is willing to pay an average price for a good company or a low price for an okay company, but you're unlikely to find it paying a really low price for a poor company.

Co-managers Kent Simons (since 1981) and Lawrence Marx III (since 1988) have put together an eye-popping long-term record that's a leader in the growth and income category, even though the fund doesn't always outperform the S&P 500. It has assumed above-average risk over fairly long periods of time, but its strengths outweigh its weaknesses, and it should be considered a core holding that's a fine alternative to the S&P 500. It will lag when growth investing is hot, but over the long run it has stayed competitive with the market.

Neuberger & Berman's ten-year annualized return of 14.86 percent through 1995 trailed the S&P 500 by 0.02 of a percentage point. That put it in the upper 10 percent of growth and income funds. A $10,000 investment would have grown to $39,974 over the ten-year period. Average risk. This no-load fund has an annual expense ratio of 0.80 percent. Ticker symbol is NGUAX. Minimum initial purchase is $1,000, or $250 for IRAs. From Neuberger & Berman Group, New York, 800-877-9700.

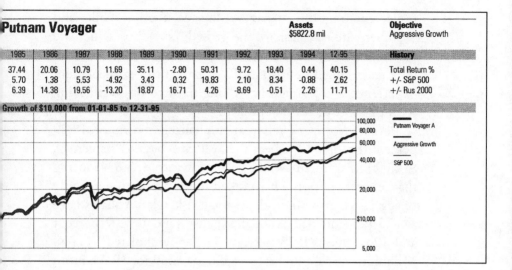

	1985	1986	1987	1988	1989	1990	1991	1992	1993	1994	12-95	History
	37.44	20.06	10.79	11.69	35.11	-2.80	50.31	9.72	18.40	0.44	40.15	Total Return %
	5.70	1.38	5.53	-4.92	3.43	0.32	19.83	2.10	8.34	-0.88	2.62	+/- S&P 500
	6.39	14.38	19.56	-13.20	18.87	16.71	4.26	-8.69	-0.51	2.26	11.71	+/- Rus 2000

Putnam Voyager

Assets
$5822.8 mil

Objective
Aggressive Growth

Growth of $10,000 from 01-01-85 to 12-31-95

Putnam Voyager A

Aggressive Growth

S&P 500

17. PUTNAM VOYAGER

It's not getting older; it's getting better. Putnam Voyager, which goes after technology, health care, and services companies with strong growth potential, has trailed the S&P 500 only four years in the past twenty. It's considered the *grande dame* of aggressive growth stock funds because for years it has been the best and most consistent entrant in its category. Currently a mid-cap fund, Voyager has held stocks such as H&R Block, Tele-Communications Inc., FlightSafety International, and Telephone & Data Systems. This is a long-term capital appreciation fund for risk-tolerant investors who like their chances with a proven winner and an important flagship product for Putnam.

The fund does, however, have a new management team in Charles Swanberg (since 1994), Roland Gillis (1995), and Robert Beck (1995), following the retirement of respected longtime manager Matt Weatherbie. Gillis and Swanberg are in charge of the growth portfolios, which are distinguished by market capitalization, while Beck handles the "fallen-angel" portfolio. They have prior management experience and Putnam has a long track record of thriving with this sort of team approach.

Putnam Voyager's ten-year annualized return of 18.29 percent through 1995 beat the S&P 500 by 3.41 percent. A $10,000 investment would have grown to $53,634 during that ten-year period. That ranked in the fifteenth percentile of aggressive growth funds. Average risk. Class A shares have a 5.75 percent load. Annual expense ratio is 1.07 percent and 12b-1 fee is 0.25 percent. Ticker symbol is PVOYX. Minimum initial purchase is $500, or $250 for IRAs. From Putnam Mutual Funds, Boston, 800-225-1581.

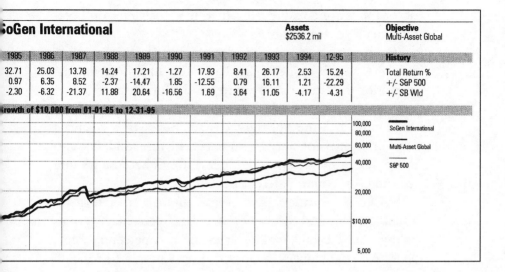

SoGen International											Assets $2536.2 mil	Objective Multi-Asset Global
1985	1986	1987	1988	1989	1990	1991	1992	1993	1994	12-95		History
32.71	25.03	13.78	14.24	17.21	-1.27	17.93	8.41	26.17	2.53	15.24		Total Return %
0.97	6.35	8.52	-2.37	-14.47	1.85	-12.55	0.79	16.11	1.21	-22.29		+/- S&P 500
-2.30	-6.32	-21.37	11.88	20.64	-16.56	1.69	3.64	11.05	-4.17	-4.31		+/- SB Wld

Growth of $10,000 from 01-01-85 to 12-31-95

- SoGen International
- Multi-Asset Global
- S&P 500

18. SOGEN INTERNATIONAL

This multi-asset global fund in some ways is like GAM International, in that it's willing to own any kind of security and doesn't worry about the world indexes. But SoGen International is much more likely to make a shrewd move and jump out quickly again after the money's been made. Portfolio manager Jean-Marie Eveillard (since 1979) is one of the few managers around who is willing to buy virtually anything, no matter how detested it is, if it's cheap enough and a gamble seems justified in his eyes. That sounds risky, but if you have enough securities with different sorts of risks, they actually diversify away risk. He is a very careful, conservative buyer. Eveillard has had only one down year since he took over the fund, and that 1.27 percent loss in 1990 was better than virtually any other domestic or foreign index. He is profiled in the chapter on port-folio manager legends.

Foreign stocks and bonds, domestic stocks and bonds, or gold are all fair game as SoGen International scours the world for the latest opportunities. This fund is an excellent core holding because it has appreciation potential like a stock fund but the volatility characteristics of a balanced fund. It would not only be an excellent first fund, but also makes sense if you own a number of funds because it's sure to bring something different to the party.

SoGen International's ten-year annualized return of 13.62 percent through 1995 was 1.26 percentage points below the S&P 500, ranking it in the first percentile of its peers. A $10,000 investment would have grown to $35,845 during that ten-year period. Below-average risk. It has a 3.75 percent load. Annual expense ratio is 1.26 percent and its 12b-1 fee is 0.25 percent. Ticker symbol is SGENX. Minimum initial purchase is $1,000. From Société Générale Asset Management, New York, 800-628-0252.

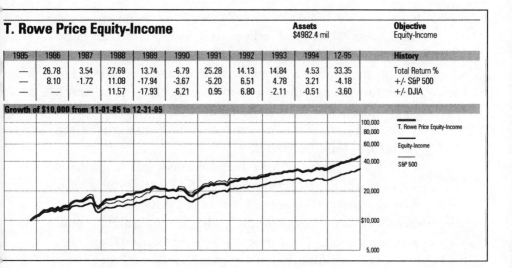

T. Rowe Price Equity-Income									Assets $4982.4 mil			Objective Equity-Income

1985	1986	1987	1988	1989	1990	1991	1992	1993	1994	12-95	History
—	26.78	3.54	27.69	13.74	-6.79	25.28	14.13	14.84	4.53	33.35	Total Return %
—	8.10	-1.72	11.08	-17.94	-3.67	-5.20	6.51	4.78	3.21	-4.18	+/- S&P 500
—	—	—	11.57	-17.93	-6.21	0.95	6.80	-2.11	-0.51	-3.60	+/- DJIA

Growth of $10,000 from 11-01-85 to 12-31-95

T. Rowe Price Equity-Income
Equity-Income
S&P 500

19. T. ROWE PRICE EQUITY-INCOME

It's a classic, an equity-income fund with 75 percent or more of its portfolio in stocks. We're talking mostly big, mature U.S. stocks with a good yield, but not particularly cheap on a statistical basis. It's tilted toward energy, utilities, financials, and higher-yielding groups, and away from growth sectors such as technology or cyclical companies that might cut dividends. Companies such as Philip Morris, Exxon, the U.K.'s SmithKline Beecham, and Honeywell have been major holdings. You'd have to go a long way down its portfolio list to find a company that most investors aren't familiar with.

An equity-income fund is supposed to pay out a yield that's slightly better than the S&P 500 after expenses, while being more conservative and less volatile. T. Rowe Price Equity-Income does just that. Portfolio manager Brian

179

Rogers (since 1985) also invests in some fixed-income securities to spice up the fund's payout. He's more than gutsy enough to buy truly ugly positions and hold them for a long time as he awaits an improvement in their condition. His knack for finding value was evident when he bought health care stocks before they rebounded. He also purchased retail stocks and real estate investment trusts (REITs) after the market had punished them.

T. Rowe Price Equity-Income's ten-year annualized return of 15.06 percent through 1995 beat the S&P 500 by 0.18 of a percentage point. That ranked it in the top 1 percent of equity-income funds. A $10,000 investment would have grown to $40,663 over that ten-year period. Low risk. It is a no-load fund. Annual expense ratio is 0.88 percent. Ticker symbol is PRFDX. Minimum initial purchase is $2,500, or $1,000 for IRAs. From T. Rowe Price Associates, Baltimore, 800-638-5660.

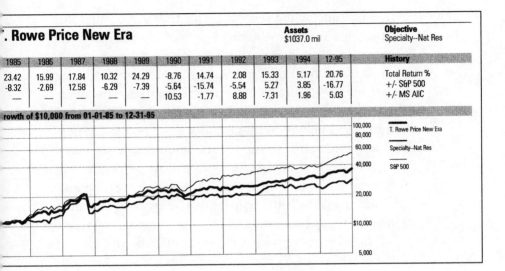

											Assets $1037.0 mil	Objective Specialty--Nat Res

. Rowe Price New Era

1985	1986	1987	1988	1989	1990	1991	1992	1993	1994	12-95	History
23.42	15.99	17.84	10.32	24.29	-8.76	14.74	2.08	15.33	5.17	20.76	Total Return %
-8.32	-2.69	12.58	-6.29	-7.39	-5.64	-15.74	-5.54	5.27	3.85	-16.77	+/- S&P 500
—	—	—	—	—	10.53	-1.77	8.88	-7.31	1.96	5.03	+/- MS AIIC

rowth of $10,000 from 01-01-85 to 12-31-95

100,000
80,000
60,000 — T. Rowe Price New Era
40,000 — Specialty--Nat Res
20,000 — S&P 500
$10,000
5,000

20. T. ROWE PRICE NEW ERA

You say you're fascinated by natural resources but too chicken to invest? This fund's for you. T. Rowe Price New Era is a diversified natural resources fund that holds energy, metals, paper companies, and gold. Names have included Mobil, Newmont Mining, and Kimberly-Clark. It will also toss in an occasional non–natural-resources stock such as Wal-Mart Stores, a top holding for years. Bristol-Myers Squibb is another example. Portfolio manager George Roche (since 1979) recently had about 90 percent of the fund in stocks, with the rest in cash, although he'll sometimes hold some bonds. This conservative version of a natural resources fund can give you exposure to rising commodity prices and also serve as a bit of an inflation hedge.

In the third quarter of 1990 when the Persian Gulf conflict and war began, T. Rowe Price New Era declined 6.5

percent in value, while the Vanguard Index 500 Fund lost 13.8 percent. And that Vanguard decline was actually considerably less than that of most other funds at the time. Roche boosted the fund's holdings in gold stocks after they sold off in 1994, anticipating a rise in the precious metal. When technology stocks took a hit in early 1996, New Era's gold and energy holdings did well. The fund generally does best relative to the natural resources group when fuel prices are in a slump, since most of its peers have big energy stakes. It can, however, lag when energy booms. This fund is held in Morningstar's 401(k) retirement plan as an inflation-hedge option.

T. Rowe Price New Era's ten-year annualized return of 11.36 percent was 3.52 percentage points less than the S&P 500. That put it in the top 11 percent of natural resources funds. A $10,000 investment would have grown to $29,336 over the ten-year period. Below-average risk. It is a no-load fund. Annual expense ratio is 0.80 percent. Ticker symbol is PRNEX. Minimum initial purchase is $2,500, or $1,000 for an IRA. From T. Rowe Price Associates, Baltimore, 800-638-5660.

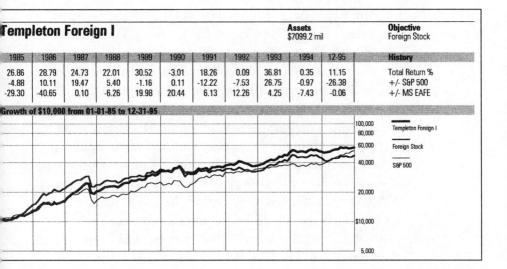

Templeton Foreign I

Assets $7099.2 mil

Objective Foreign Stock

	1985	1986	1987	1988	1989	1990	1991	1992	1993	1994	12-95	History
	26.86	28.79	24.73	22.01	30.52	-3.01	18.26	0.09	36.81	0.35	11.15	Total Return %
	-4.88	10.11	19.47	5.40	-1.16	0.11	-12.22	-7.53	26.75	-0.97	-26.38	+/- S&P 500
	-29.30	-40.65	0.10	-6.26	19.98	20.44	6.13	12.26	4.25	-7.43	-0.06	+/- MS EAFE

Growth of $10,000 from 01-01-85 to 12-31-95

- Templeton Foreign I
- Foreign Stock
- S&P 500

21. TEMPLETON FOREIGN

Giant Temple Foreign is a much purer international play than the considerably more diverse GAM International or SoGen International, yet it's not merely an index-like fund. Like all Templeton funds, it seeks value, has low portfolio turnover, and tends to stay away from higher-priced markets when it doesn't agree with their price tags. It has outperformed the average international stock fund for nine consecutive years and its risk levels are below those of the average general equity fund. Portfolio manager Mark Holowesko (since 1987) emphasizes large-capitalization stocks and has had a heavy weighting in financials, industrial cyclicals, and consumer durables.

Holowesko stayed completely out of the Japanese market when he considered it overpriced, preferring the opportunities in other Pacific Rim nations, Europe, and

Latin America. His portfolio has included U.S. Treasury notes, Telefónica de España, ANZ Banking Group, and Volvo. He usually doesn't pick up the trendier stock groups, such as technology, until they've taken a downward slide. This is a core international fund that benefits greatly from Templeton's worldwide research team.

Templeton Foreign's ten-year annualized return of 16.37 percent through 1995 beat the S&P 500 by 3.57 percentage points. It ranked in the upper 4 percent of foreign stock funds. A $10,000 investment would have grown to $39,634 over the ten-year period. Below-average risk. Class I shares have a 5.75 percent load. Annual expense ratio is 1.15 percent and 12b-1 fee is 0.25 percent. Ticker symbol is TEMFX. Minimum initial purchase is $100, with no minimum for IRAs. From Franklin Templeton Group, San Mateo, California, 800-292-9293.

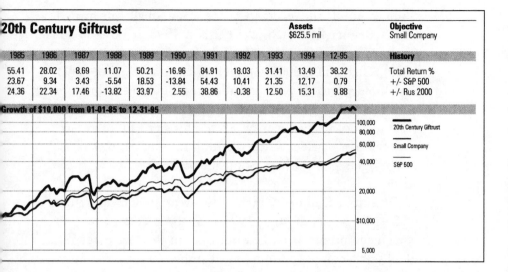

20th Century Giftrust											Assets $625.5 mil	Objective Small Company
1985	1986	1987	1988	1989	1990	1991	1992	1993	1994	12-95		History
55.41	28.02	8.69	11.07	50.21	-16.96	84.91	18.03	31.41	13.49	38.32		Total Return %
23.67	9.34	3.43	-5.54	18.53	-13.84	54.43	10.41	21.35	12.17	0.79		+/- S&P 500
24.36	22.34	17.46	-13.82	33.97	2.55	38.86	-0.38	12.50	15.31	9.88		+/- Rus 2000

Growth of $10,000 from 01-01-85 to 12-31-95

- 20th Century Giftrust
- Small Company
- S&P 500

22. TWENTIETH CENTURY GIFTRUST

This fund is the ticket to your child's education. Set up as a trust, it can be given as a gift to an individual or organization and can't be redeemed for ten years, or until the shareholder (if a child) reaches the age of maturity. The restrictive nature of this arrangement lets the fund pursue aggressive strategies without fear of having shareholders panic and cash in. It has also kept investors from pouring large amounts of money into the fund at one time, so its smaller asset size has enabled it to continue investing in small-company stocks.

Twentieth Century Giftrust is an extremely powerful and volatile fund. It takes off like a cannonball in a bull market, though it can take a quick hit when the market or a sector turns bad. Its long-term returns have been aston-

185

ishingly good, and even in years when small-cap growth stocks weren't hot, such as 1992 and 1993, it posted solid gains. Co-portfolio managers James Stowers III (since 1983), Glenn Fogle (1993), and James Starks (since 1993) have boldly moved into volatile areas such as technology when they felt the prices were right. Its returns symbolize what technology has been able to do for some funds' returns over the past decade. When the fund stumbles, it picks itself up and gets going again. Soon it's back up to warp speed again.

Twentieth Century Giftrust's ten-year annualized return of 24.12 percent through 1995 beat the S&P 500 by 9.24 percentage points. It ranked not only in the first percentile of all small-company funds, but had the top ten-year annualized return of the more than 7,000 funds in the Morningstar database. A $10,000 investment would have grown to $86,721 over that ten-year period. High risk. It is a no-load fund with 0.98 percent annual expense ratio. Ticker symbol is TWGTX. Minimum initial purchase is $250. From Twentieth Century Investors, Kansas City, Missouri, 800-345-2021.

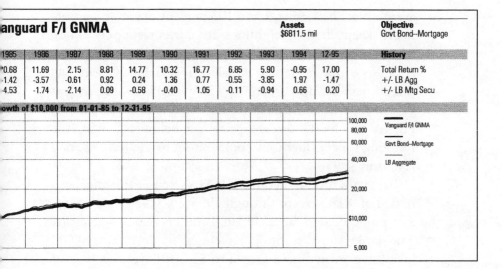

anguard F/I GNMA									Assets $6811.5 mil		Objective Govt Bond--Mortgage
1985	1986	1987	1988	1989	1990	1991	1992	1993	1994	12-95	History
*0.68	11.69	2.15	8.81	14.77	10.32	16.77	6.85	5.90	-0.95	17.00	Total Return %
-1.42	-3.57	-0.61	0.92	0.24	1.36	0.77	-0.55	-3.85	1.97	-1.47	+/- LB Agg
-4.53	-1.74	-2.14	0.09	-0.58	-0.40	1.05	-0.11	-0.94	0.66	0.20	+/- LB Mtg Secu

owth of $10,000 from 01-01-85 to 12-31-95

100,000
80,000
60,000
40,000

Vanguard F/I GNMA

Govt Bond--Mortgage

LB Aggregate

20,000

$10,000

5,000

23. VANGUARD FIXED-INCOME SECURITIES GNMA

One of the real keys to the success of this government mortgage fund is Vanguard's minuscule annual expense ratio of 0.30 percent, which gives it a leg up over competitors. Its risk-to-reward profile is also one of the most attractive in its group. The fund has never lost money in a calendar year except for its decline of less than 1 percent in 1994, which was the worst bond market in sixty years. It's a high-grade bond fund, a first choice for someone who wants a bond fund. A second choice for a portfolio might be Kemper High-Yield Bond.

Vanguard Fixed-Income Securities GNMA generally is close to fully invested in thirty-year single-family pass-throughs, the most common type of mortgage bond. Portfolio manager Paul Kaplan tries to keep the fund's averge price between 99 and 103 percent of par, so he normally keeps large weightings in current-coupon issues. This doesn't erode capital, keeps it in a steady market, and, if rates go down, it will actually grow a bit. Kaplan will sometimes alter his core strategy in special instances, such as in late 1994 when he decided that interest rates had peaked. He let the fund's average price fall below par, with the resulting longer durations contributing to the fund's strong results in 1995.

Vanguard Fixed-Income GNMA's ten-year annualized return of 9.18 percent through 1995 was 0.45 of a percentage point below the Lehman Brothers Index aggregate. This ranked in the top 1 percent of its peers. A $10,000 investment would have grown to $24,070 over the 10-year period. Below-average risk. This is a no-load fund with an annual expense ratio of 0.30 percent. Ticker symbol is VFIIX. Minimum initial purchase is $3,000, or $500 for IRAs. From Vanguard Group, Valley Forge, Pennsylvania, 800-662-7447.

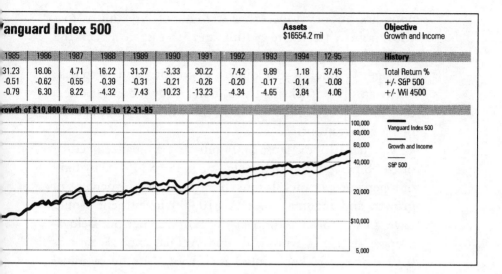

| Vanguard Index 500 | | | | | | | | | | | Assets $16554.2 mil | Objective Growth and Income |

1985	1986	1987	1988	1989	1990	1991	1992	1993	1994	12-95	History
31.23	18.06	4.71	16.22	31.37	-3.33	30.22	7.42	9.89	1.18	37.45	Total Return %
-0.51	-0.62	-0.55	-0.39	-0.31	-0.21	-0.26	-0.20	-0.17	-0.14	-0.08	+/- S&P 500
-0.79	6.30	8.22	-4.32	7.43	10.23	-13.23	-4.34	-4.65	3.84	4.06	+/- Wil 4500

Growth of $10,000 from 01-01-85 to 12-31-95

24. VANGUARD INDEX TRUST 500

This is the fund that has proved over the past twenty years of its existence that there's a lot to be said for stock indexing. If you were to own only one fund, this one would certainly be well worth considering. Vanguard Group, profiled in the chapter on fund families, is owned by fund shareholders, so it can provide management at cost. Vanguard Index Trust 500 has an annual expense ratio of just 0.19 percent, compared to 1.3 percent for the average domestic stock fund. That's a tremendous advantage. Meanwhile, portfolio manager George "Gus" Sauter (since 1987) keeps improving trading systems to manage money more efficiently, and the fund's enormous assets means it can realize economies of scale through big block trades and negotiated lower commissions.

Over time, the fund has been very successful in compounding money. One other strength of indexing is that you know what you're getting and it's easy to check the fund's progress. You don't have to worry about the fund manager suddenly deciding to go off and purchase Peruvian silver stocks that you didn't know about. It offers investors a piece of the action in the world's largest economy at a bargain price.

Vanguard Index Trust 500's ten-year annualized return of 14.58 percent through 1995 trailed the S&P 500 by 0.30 of a percentage point. It ranked in the upper 14 percent of growth and income funds. A $10,000 investment would have grown to $39,007 over the ten-year period. Below-average risk. It is a no-load fund. Annual expense ratio is 0.19 percent. Ticker symbol is VFINX. Minimum initial purchase is $3,000, or $500 for IRAs. From Vanguard Group, Valley Forge, Pennsylvania, 800-662-7447.

anguard Muni High-Yield											Assets $1960.8 mil	Objective Muni Bond--National
1985	1986	1987	1988	1989	1990	1991	1992	1993	1994	12-95		History
21.65	19.67	-1.57	13.81	11.07	5.91	14.75	9.88	12.66	-5.07	18.09		Total Return %
-0.45	4.41	-4.33	5.92	-3.46	-3.05	-1.25	2.48	2.91	-2.15	-0.38		+/- LB Agg
1.63	0.35	-3.07	3.65	0.28	-1.39	2.61	1.06	0.38	0.07	0.63		+/- LB Muni

rowth of $10,000 from 01-01-85 to 12-31-95

Vanguard Muni High-Yield
Muni Bond--National
LB Aggregate

25. VANGUARD MUNICIPAL HIGH-YIELD

Don't let the name fool you. This isn't junk. This high-yield fund isn't really a low-credit fund, but primarily investment grade. It has only about 10 percent of its portfolio in nonrated bonds and 36 percent in AAA-rated bonds, so you can also consider it a peace-of-mind fund. Co-managers Ian MacKinnon (since 1981) and Jerome Jacobs (1988) favor call-protect issues and attempt to hedge out some of the fund's interest rate sensitivity by using Treasury futures.

This strategy has over time enabled management to hold longer-maturity issues while keeping the fund from being crushed by rising rates. That is not to say, however, that it will not encounter interest rate volatility. Yet most investors in municipal bonds want safety, and you won't have to

191

worry much about defaults with Vanguard Municipal High-Yield's portfolio. It's a fund that's best for investors who seek above-average returns without taking on above-average credit risk. Its annual expense ratio of 0.21 percent is a driving force behind its higher returns.

Vanguard Municipal High-Yield's ten-year annualized return of 9.65 percent through 1995 beat the Lehman Brothers Index aggregate by 0.02 of a percentage point. That ranked it in the top 2 percent of national municipal bond funds. A $10,000 investment would have grown to $25,123 over the ten-year period. Its ticker symbol is VWAHX. Above-average risk. It's a no-load fund. Annual expense ratio is 0.21 percent. Minimum initial purchase is $3,000, or $500 for IRAs. From Vanguard Group, Valley Forge, Pennsylvania, 800-662-7447.

UP-AND-COMING FUNDS

Some other top-notch funds didn't meet the longer-term performance criteria to place among the top twenty-five time-tested funds, but should nonetheless be considered by investors because their performance has been superb. They represent a broad range of different types carefully culled from the thousands of available funds.

Especially worthy of note are: (1) PBHG Growth from Pilgrim Baxter & Associates, Wayne, Pennsylvania; (2) John Hancock Special Equities from John Hancock Funds, Boston; (3) Oppenheimer Quest Opportunity Value Fund from Oppenheimer Funds, Denver; (4) T. Rowe Price Equity-Income from T. Rowe Price Associates, Baltimore; (5) Baron Asset from Baron Capital, New York; (6) T. Rowe Price International Bond; (7) Putnam New Opportunities from Putnam Mutual Funds, Boston; (8) Evergreen Foundation from Evergreen Asset Management, New York; (9) Fidelity Stock Selector from Fidelity Group, Boston; and (10) Strong Government Securities from Strong Capital Management, Milwaukee, Wisconsin.

Other solid contenders include (11) Smallcap World from American Funds, Los Angeles; (12) Longleaf Partners from Southeastern Asset Management, Memphis; (13) Merrill Lynch Global Allocation from Merrill Lynch Asset Management, New York; (14) Kaufmann from Edgemont Asset Management, New York; (15) Janus Flexible Income from Janus Capital, Denver; (16) Invesco Total Return from Invesco Funds Group, Denver; (17) Harbor Capital Appreciation from Harbor Capital Advisors, Toledo, Ohio; (18) Alger Growth Portfolio from Fred Alger Management, New York; (19) Third Avenue Value from EQSF Advisers, New York; and (20) Capital Income Builder from American Funds, Los Angeles.

DOWN AND OUT

Lest all this talk about wonderfully performing mutual funds gets you to thinking that you can blindly come up with a winner, perhaps you should consider the other side of the coin. Some mutual funds are outright losers for long periods of time. The reasons for their ongoing woes are usually high expenses, poor strategies for volatile growth stocks, and generally inept management. Some funds are quietly folded or merged into other funds by big mutual fund companies. In some cases, the worst-performing funds are actually owned by the portfolio manager, which explains why they're able to continue on their way without anyone getting fired. While the past may not be an infallible indicator of the future, truly terrible performance in the past is a red warning light for what's ahead.

Perhaps the very worst-performing mutual funds of all have been those owned and run by Charles Steadman of Washington, D.C. They've dwindled over decades of terrible returns to a point where probably only family money is still included in their assets. They pioneered risky futures and options strategies before anyone else considered them, they had high expenses, and they made poor management decisions. It's difficult to even obtain a list of their portfolio holdings these days. How bad are they? The Steadman Technology Growth Fund suffered an annualized loss of 13.98 percent over the ten-year period through 1995 to rank dead last among all growth funds. Meanwhile, the Steadman American Industry Fund had a ten-year annualized loss of 12.05 percent. Yep, that was good for last place in the growth and income category. Nearly as bad have been Steadman Investment Fund and Steadman Associated Fund. I'll spare you the negative performance numbers.

Another dismal performer has been the American Heritage Fund of New York, a poor-performing, high-risk fund taken over by portfolio manager Heiko Thieme in

1990. He had a couple of years of strong performance, but then the bottom fell out once again as some of his small-company strategies bombed. The fund's ten-year annualized loss through 1995 was 4.76 percent to rank in the lower ninety-sixth percentile of all aggressive growth funds.

Among other consistent losers despite the opportunities from a raging bull market have been 44 Wall Street Equity of New York, with a ten-year annualized return of 7.73 percent; Rainbow Fund of New York, with a ten-year annualized return of 6.88 percent; Security Ultra of Topeka, Kansas, with a ten-year annualized return of 6.08 percent; National Industries of Englewood, Colorado, with a ten-year annualized return of 9.60 percent; and Value Line Special Situations, with a ten-year annualized return of 8.47 percent.

With those sobering returns to consider, it's obvious that it still does pay to do your homework, to check track records, and to carefully monitor your mutual fund holdings. Even if you don't exactly pick all winners, you'll certainly be likely to avoid outright disasters as you put together an intelligent portfolio of funds. So that's your reality check. May there be no Steadman-style returns in your investment future to crack the foundation of your investment castle.

CHAPTER 11

■

MYTHS OF A DIFFERENT COLOR

"Don't let anyone tell you that you just won't understand an investment. If you're already spending time tracking mutual funds, it can be lucrative and worthwhile to extend the effort to related vehicles."
— CATHERINE GILLIS ODELBO, PUBLISHER
OF MORNINGSTAR EQUITIES GROUP

Investment myths go beyond mutual funds.

Misconceptions abound regarding variable annuities, those modern retirement vehicles that have grown in popularity by offering countless mutual fund portfolios; closed-end funds, which are the close relatives of conventional open-end mutual funds but traded on regular stock exchanges; and stocks, a primary investment component of mutual funds.

Morningstar's ongoing research into all three of those

vehicles for its print and electronic products seeks to explode stubborn myths while expanding investor knowledge. A first step, of course, is understanding what they're all about.

A variable annuity is a product offered by insurance companies, broker-dealers, financial planners, and the companies themselves that permits you to invest in a wide range of mutual fund portfolios and defer accumulated earnings until you begin to withdraw your money. That's most likely when you're retired and in a lower tax bracket. It's an opportunity to invest your money with some of the investment world's most successful mutual fund companies, your return depending on how the funds you select perform. The size of your account at retirement depends on your investment acumen.

A closed-end fund, unlike a conventional open-end mutual fund that issues unlimited amounts of shares and redeems them on demand, issues only a fixed number of shares at an initial public offering. These shares are then traded on the New York, American, or NASDAQ exchanges just like those of any public company. Shares are bought through a stockbroker, and regular brokerage commissions must be paid. As with any equity, the fund's share price on the exchange will fluctuate based upon its popularity and general market trends. That market price may differ from the net asset value (NAV) of all the securities in its portfolio. As a result, it's sometimes possible to buy assets for less than their true value, while other times you wind up paying more. A fund selling for a stock price higher than its NAV is trading at a premium, while a fund selling for a price lower than its NAV is trading at a discount. Premiums usually don't last long, since they indicate that the fund is selling for more than its portfolio is actually worth. Obviously, most investors try to buy their closed-end funds at a discount.

Stocks, of course, are not only the heart and soul of many mutual funds, but an investment worth studying on their own. In addition, the number of U.S. investors buying stocks of foreign companies has risen significantly in the 1990s, with the value of foreign stock owned by Americans surpassing the value of U.S. shares held by foreigners for the first time ever. Just because stocks have obviously been around a long time doesn't mean they're either old hat or too complicated for average folks. What you don't know about stocks can hurt you and your pocketbook.

Here are more investment myths that, based upon Morningstar research, are worth exploding:

Myth No. 1: Because the mutual funds contained within variable annuities are the same as mutual funds sold directly to the public, it's convenient to look up their returns in the newspaper.

Big mistake. Even if they're from the same fund company and bear similar names, the variable annuity mutual fund by law must be a different pool of assets than a conventional mutual fund. These two types of funds are also likely to have different returns and perhaps even different managers. Exactly how distinctive each is in performance depends on who is managing it, how similar the funds are designed to be, and their respective asset sizes, Morningstar has found. Investors must take time to know the variable annuity fund and see if the performance difference is something they're comfortable with.

For example, variable annuity Dreyfus Small-Cap Variable Investment Fund and the mutual fund Dreyfus New Leaders appear to be quite alike and both are run by manager Tom Frank, but the annuity has handily outperformed the fund. Portfolio manager Richard Hoey's two portfolios, Dreyfus Growth & Income mutual fund and Dreyfus Variable Investment Growth & Income, have had significantly different returns. The variable annuity fund did much better. Meanwhile, the Fidelity Equity-Income Fund and the variable annuity Fidelity VIP Fund Equity-Income actually have different managers. Always do research into the track record of the specific fund offered in the annuity, not the fund after which it was cloned.

Myth No. 2: Variable annuities are twice as expensive as conventional mutual funds.

Not necessarily. A number of variable annuity products are quite competitively priced, with a very minor difference in annual cost of only .30 to .50 percent above conventional mutual funds. While it's true that grossly overpriced variable annuities might be as much as 2 percent higher than a comparable mutual fund, those are extreme examples. The average U.S. diversified stock fund has an annual expense ratio of 1.37 percent, while the average variable annuity with a similar portfolio has an annual expense ratio of 2.04 percent. Included in the latter are the insurance expenses that pay for annuity features such as the guaranteed death benefit, ensuring that if you die during the annuity's accumulation years, the value to your beneficiary will be at least as much as you put into it.

Myth No. 3: A variable annuity is a great product for passing money along to your children when you pass away.

No way. The variable annuity is taxed and structured to be used at retirement and is ineffective in estate planning. That's because when you die, your family would have to pay all the owed income taxes on your gains, unlike a regular insurance policy, which passes the money along tax-free. Use other instruments to pass money to your children. This is a retirement vehicle and should be used only that way. Otherwise, you'll be giving away a lot of your family's hard-earned savings to Uncle Sam.

Myth No. 4: The way you make money in closed-end funds is to buy them at discounts and sell them at premiums.

There's no guarantee that you'll make money if you buy a closed-end fund at a discount and sell it at a premium. Fluctuations in the underlying net asset value of the closed-end fund notwithstanding, what matters is what the market price has done during the time you've owned it. Investors tend to get too caught up in the premiums and discounts of closed-end funds as they seek bargains. It's better to think of your closed-end fund just as you would a stock. After all, you've either made money or you haven't. Consider the New Age Media Fund, which began and ended 1995 selling at a 20 percent discount to its NAV. The fund increased 45 percent in value during the year for its shareholders. Obviously, the discount didn't matter at all to those happy folks who made money. Clearly, there can be advantages to a strategy of buying at discounts and selling at premiums. But investors who base their closed-end investing solely on this principle could be cutting themselves off from some of the best opportunities the closed-end universe has to offer.

Myth No. 5: Closed-end funds are always much more volatile than conventional open-end funds.

An incorrect blanket statement. There's really nothing inherently more volatile about the nature of a closed-end fund. What is true is that more closed-end funds than open-end funds are invested in volatile markets. For example, Turkey, Pakistan, and Mexico have their own closed-end funds. If you were to instead take a regular blue-chip U.S. closed-end fund and compare it to an open-end counterpart with similar holdings, you wouldn't find any difference in volatility at all.

Myth No. 6: Stocks are too difficult for most people to understand, which is why average investors should always stick with mutual funds.

Despite headlines on magazine covers about mutual funds being the answer to all of your prayers, investors should try to understand all investments and rationally decide which fit best into their personal portfolios. Mutual funds provide incredible diversity, and, when chosen properly, large rewards. Yet a stock provides a greater opportunity to pinpoint exactly what you're investing in because it represents a specific company with products or services that you can scrutinize personally. You're buying your own stock, no one's making the decision for you, and you needn't analyze what's going on inside a portfolio manager's mind.

With a mutual fund, it's difficult to make ten times your money because of the automatic diversification among so many stocks. However, the "right" individual stock can really take off like a rocket. Mutual funds and individual stocks can coexist quite well in your personal portfolio and you should be able to understand how both of them function. Having a grasp of individual stocks is also a definite plus in better understanding the holdings in your mutual funds. A look at the types of stocks a fund holds will give you a quick idea of the underlying strategy and performance of the fund.

Myth No. 7: Currency fluctuations and political risk make investing in foreign stocks an arduous task.

If you're a long-term investor, which you definitely should be, forget about all of those excuses to avoid international holdings. Sir John Templeton, founder of the Templeton Funds, proved that currency fluctuations tend to even themselves out over a full market cycle of five to ten years. Similarly, political risks usually aren't what they're cracked up to be, and they too even out over time. What matters is whether the company makes money and whether its stock price goes up as a result, not all of those big-picture concerns that no mortal can effectively hope to control anyway. In the modern world, companies are competing against one another, not against other countries. Investors from other parts of the world are already adept at spreading their holdings around the globe, but this intelligent diversification concept remains relatively new to U.S. investors.

VARIABLE ANNUITIES

Understand the basics of all these investments. For example, annuities are basically contracts with an insurance company. In return for a lump-sum purchase payment today or making several subsequent payments, you'll receive a stream of payments from the company in the future. There's also the death benefit that protects against investment loss at the time of death. Over time, a well-managed variable annuity should handily outperform a fixed annuity. Selection of a variable annuity involves selection of a subaccount with a proven track record and good prospects for the future. The annuity owner follows the accumulation unit value (AUV), which is calculated by measuring the change in value of the investment, adding the portfolio's income and realized capital gains, and subtracting the management and insurance expenses. It's similar to the net asset value of a mutual fund.

Remember that variable annuities are different from traditional fixed annuities, in which your account grows at a fixed rate of interest until you begin to withdraw your money. In addition, unlike fixed annuities, variable annuity subaccounts are legally separate from the insurance company's general accounts, and your funds therefore won't be

lost or frozen if the company fails. But if you aren't confident about dealing with the volatility of the stock market,
don't select a variable annuity. The conservative investor
who just cashed out of a certificate of deposit may not be
ready to add to his or her risk tolerance. When investing
in an annuity, be sure you can afford to leave your money
in until age fifty-nine and a half, because early withdrawals
can be expensive. The Internal Revenue Service exacts
taxes and a 10 percent penalty on the accumulated earnings. There's usually a surrender charge as well. As a result,
variable annuities aren't for people who don't have time
horizons of ten years or more. A variable annuity should
be considered just one part of a complete plan for your
retirement. First look into choices that offer the greatest tax
advantages, which might be 401(k) plans, individual retirement accounts, or Keogh plans for the self-employed.
Unlike these plans, though, variable annuities allow unlimited contributions.

Variable annuities have grown from $129 billion in assets
at the end of 1991 to more than $240 billion today, mostly
as a result of hitching their wagon to the rising mutual fund
star. They range from those with a few subaccount choices to those with a wide spectrum of selections. While several years ago the average variable annuity had about five
non-money-market options, the average is now nine and
some have as many as eighteen choices. Firms not only
offer their own funds, but a number of others from well-
known mutual fund firms in order to give a number of
solid choices. Performance obviously differs, so you must
use the same judicious method in selecting a variable annuity and subaccount as you would a conventional mutual
fund. Transferring income-tax-free between various variable annuity products is fairly easy through what's called a
1035 exchange (named for the tax code permitting it),
though you'll have to pay surrender charges from your old
annuity when they apply. The variable annuity industry has

been cannibalizing older, less investment-wise accounts as the assets of newer offerings have grown. In fact, nearly one-third of new variable annuity account dollars come from other existing variable annuities. Smart investors obviously figure out which are the best deals.

"One great thing about variable annuities is that all of the variable funds are available for the taking by different companies, so they can determine, for example, who has a terrific international fund and can then put it into their own product pipelines without having to create an entirely new fund," observed Jennifer Strickland, editor of *Morningstar Variable Annuities/Life*, who has directed the firm's annuity research through its binder product that tracks 958 subaccounts and its Principia software product that follows 3,700 subaccounts. "As a result, there are a lot of products available with strong track records and high-quality managers, such as Shelby Davis, Ralph Wanger, and Dick Strong."

Some funds are available in many different variable annuities offered by a number of companies. For example, Fidelity VIP Fund Equity-Income is offered in nearly fifty variable annuities and Alger American Fund Growth Portfolio is available in twenty-two variable annuities. That means investors can pick the funds they like best and then shop around for the variable annuities that offer them the best features at the best price.

While the traditional variable annuity is sold through insurance agents, broker-dealers, and financial planners, a growing trend is the no-load variable annuity. Sold directly to the public by the company itself or through fee-only financial planners, the no-load variable annuity usually has no surrender charge and a lower annual charge. As a result, it offers greater liquidity through increased ability to exchange assets through 1035 exchanges and also means you pay less each year. Though still a relatively small portion of the overall business, the concept has behind it some of the giant mutual fund companies. Best of all, low fees calm investors' nagging fears that variable annuities are overpriced investments. Morningstar research, however, found a number of traditional variable annuities that don't cost that much more, based on annual fees, than the new no-load variable annuities. It searched out those with insurance-expense ratios (including percentage-based contract charges) of 1.25 percent or less and ignored surrender charges because they can be avoided entirely by sticking with the investment. To cut down the list further, it also removed "qualified-only" variable annuities that are used in teacher, physician, and nonprofit benefit plans. Some of these variable annuities met both the expense and performance criteria while beating the no-load Vanguard Variable Annuity Equity Index over a three-year period. That's proof that no-loads aren't the only variable annuities that offer value.

In its variable annuities work, Morningstar has been critical of shareholder reports in much the same way it has critiqued those of conventional mutual funds. Variable annuity shareholder reports are clearly not all that they should be. Most fail to be the candid and timely mode of communication they're intended to be. Dry prose, weak organization, and only vague reference to current strategies have rendered many of them virtually meaningless. Although firms have sixty days from the end of the period to send the shareholder report to investors, in the past some have stretched that time limit. A good shareholder report should educate and, in doing so, demonstrate a company's concern for the investor's financial well-being. Equitable's Hudson River Trust, for example, includes portfolio detail and insight into the manager's thinking. Shareholder reports of Fidelity's VIP funds include several key portfolio facts and a manager interview that details how the manager is reacting to market conditions. Such quality reports are also willing to tackle touchy subjects such as disappointing performance or managerial changes.

Is a variable annuity primarily insurance or an investment? The insurance industry's stance has long been that variable annuities and variable life are insurance products first and investments second. That position was necessary to convince Congress and the Treasury Department to preserve variable products' favored tax treatment and to react against misleading sales practices that promote variable life as a personal savings account rather than life insurance. Yet the public sees variable products as investments, and no amount of arguing will change that. Rather than admitting that variable products walk a tightrope between insurance and investment, those companies have favored the insurance side and downplayed the investments. Variable insurance customers, however, are both investors and insurance clients. Those companies that respect the investor in their clients are most likely to offer appealing variable annuities.

NO-LOAD VARIABLE ANNUITIES
SOLD DIRECTLY TO PUBLIC

COMPANY	CONTRACT CHARGE	SURRENDER CHARGE	ANNUAL INSURANCE EXPENSE	SUB-ACCOUNTS AVAILABLE
Fidelity Retirement Reserves Fidelity Investments Life Insurance Boston 800-752-6342	$30	5 % for 5 years	1%	10
Janus Retirement Advantage Janus Capital Denver 800-504-4440	$30	None	.85%	8
Schwab Investment Advantage Charles Schwab Investment Management San Francisco 800-838-0650	$25	None	.85%	12
Scudder Horizon Plan Scudder Stevens & Clark Boston 800-242-4402	None	None	.70%	6
T. Rowe Price No Load Variety Annuity T. Rowe Price Associates Baltimore 800-469-6589	None	None	.55%	5
USAA Life Variable Annuity USAA Life San Antonio, Texas 800-531-4265	$30	None	1.15%	7
Vanguard Variable Annuity Plan Vanguard Group Valley Forge, Pennsylvania 800-562-2391	$24	None	.55%	6

208

REASONABLY PRICED VARIABLE ANNUITIES
SOLD THROUGH BROKERS

COMPANY	CONTRACT CHARGE	MAXIMUM SURRENDER CHARGE	ANNUAL INSURANCE EXPENSE	SUB-ACCOUNTS AVAILABLE
American Skandia Axiom American Skandia Life Assurance Shelton, Connecticut 800-752-6342	$35	6 % Declines over 7 years	1%	21
Connecticut Mutual Panorama Connecticut Mutual Life Insurance Hartford, Connecticut 800-343-5629	$40	5% Declines over 10 years	.73%	4
Guardian Investor Guardian Insurance & Annuity Lehigh Valley, Pennsylvania 800-221-3253	$35	6%	1.15%	9
Lincoln National Multi Fund Lincoln National Life Insurance Fort Wayne, Indiana 800-348-1212	$25	7% Declines over 7 years	1%	11
Penn Mutual Diversifier II Penn Mutual Life Insurance Philadelphia, Pennsylvania 800-548-1119	$30	7% Declines over 6 years	1.25%	15
Phoenix Home Life Big Edge Plus Phoenix Home Life Mutual Insurance Greenfield, Massachusetts .800-447-4312	$35	6% Declines over 6 years	1.25	9
Prudential Discovery Plus Prudential Insurance of America Newark, New Jersey 800-445-4571	$30	7% Declines over 7 years	1.20%	14

BEST-PERFORMING VARIABLE ANNUITY PORTFOLIOS
TO WATCH FOR

FUND NAME	3-YEAR ANNUALIZED RETURN
SAFECO Resource Series Trust Equity	20.00%
Fidelity VIP Fund Equity-Income	19.24%
Alger American Fund Growth	18.38%
Connecticut Mutual Financial Series I Growth	17.59%
Prudential Series Fund Common Stock	17.33%
Templeton Variable Product Series Stock	17.27%
Fidelity VIP Fund Growth	16.98%
TMK/United Funds Growth	16.70%
Lincoln National Social Awareness Fund	16.55%
Phoenix Edge Series Fund Growth	16.12%
Lincoln National Growth & Income Fund	15.86%
Guardian Stock Fund	15.68%

(These were the highest returns available for the 3-year period ending in 1995. Returns vary somewhat depending on the expenses of the variable annuity in which the fund is placed.)

CLOSED-END FUNDS

Most investors don't understand what closed-end funds are all about. There's a closed-end fund for virtually every financial goal, although those that invest in the stocks of a single country often grab the most limelight on those occasions when they produce dramatic returns. Others that specialize in diversified stock portfolios, specific groups such as health care, financial firms, and media, or taxable and municipal bonds are worthy of note as well. Remember that the closed-end fund shares can't be bought directly from the fund itself. After the initial offering, the fund is closed. Except under special circumstances such as rights offerings, it doesn't issue new shares and it doesn't redeem them either. Whenever a shareholder sells shares, another investor buys them, so the transaction has no impact on the fund's asset base. One advantage of a closed-end fund's fixed number of shares is that it gives its portfolio manager a stable pool of assets to invest without having to worry about raising or investing new amounts without warning. There's no rash of redemptions when times are rough. The stability of assets also makes the closed-end fund the preferred vehicle for single-country funds, since a developing country's stock market has the assurance that this large amount of foreign capital won't be removed suddenly upon shareholder request.

The multitude of available closed-end single-country funds gives investors who are looking for foreign exposure a chance to be do-it-yourselfers. They can easily construct regional portfolios that reflect their preferences more accurately than the already-constructed open- and closed-end regional funds they could buy. These reflect the strategy of the portfolio manager, not their own, as to how various economies and stock markets will perform and which nation's stocks should be included. Or, in other cases, the funds were constructed simply as indexes of the region.

"A closed-end fund is the best way, or only way, to get into many areas such as Mexico, Chile, or Ireland when you want to do more than simply own the stock of one company in a specific country," explained Gregg Wolper, editor of *Morningstar Closed-End Funds*, who directs research through the binder product covering 350 closed-end funds and Principia software product following 520 funds. "It is important to remember, however, that just because a country's market does well doesn't necessarily mean that the closed-end fund bearing its name will prosper, since portfolio management and stock selection will ultimately make the real difference. For example, there are three closed-end funds devoted to Spain and all perform differently."

Closed-end funds do have means to raise new capital even though they have a fixed number of shares. They can hold a rights offering, in which existing shareholders can purchase additional shares, usually at a discount to the fund's current market price. They may engage in leveraging, which is borrowing money from a bank or issuing preferred shares. A fund doing this hopes to earn a higher rate of return from its investments than it is paying out in interest. It may issue new shares that can be bought by new and existing shareholders. Finally, it can turn itself into an open-end mutual fund and then take in an unlimited amount of new assets.

Surprisingly, the overall asset mix among closed-end funds is tilted toward fixed-income funds, rather than the stock funds that garner most of the publicity. Of the $134 billion in closed-end funds, about $98 billion is in 353 fixed-income funds. Another $36 billion is in 145 equity funds. There are considerations worth keeping in mind as far as the costs of these vehicles are concerned. Closed-end funds are typically sold by brokers who don't charge the investor a commission. But underwriting fees and commissions come from assets raised through the sale of shares. The result is an immediate decline in net asset value that averages 8 percent, certainly not an auspicious start for an investment. Many investors in new closed-end fund shares haven't seen their shares reach the original offering price. This underscores the importance of choosing wisely.

In the early 1990s, the closed-end fund market became overblown, with a raft of emerging-market and fixed-income choices introduced. Because the devaluation of Mexico's currency in late 1994 took its toll on all emerging-market investments, the new closed-end funds were also hit hard. Despite hefty discounts, many were simply unable to attract investors. A shakeout in the industry followed and the total of closed-end funds declined. A record number were transformed into open-end mutual funds or merged with open-end funds, there were some liquidations, and the rush of new funds slowed to a trickle. However, the slowdown in closed-end initial public offerings was due more to a cyclical turn in the markets that are most suited for closed-end funds than to any fundamental problem with the closed-end structure. In many ways, the shakeout that reduced the total number of closed-end funds was positive and somewhat overdue. The market's disdain for the closed-end universe resulted in the availability of many bargains in closed-end funds.

The strategy of buying a closed-end fund at a discount to get both a bargain and protection from a decline in price has been a traditional one. But do discounts on closed-end funds really provide a protective cushion for them? To find out, Morningstar conducted a study that examined closed-end fund performance over a ten-year period. It first checked to see if discounts shielded investors from steep, sudden losses by screening for funds that suffered a quarterly NAV loss of more than 15 percent, and that had entered the quarter with a discount wider than 5 percent. In theory, the cushion should have limited the market-price losses of these funds, and their market returns should have been better than their NAV returns. While it turns out that while the discount did provide a cushion more often than not, results weren't all that impressive. Of 113 cases where these conditions existed, the market return turned out to be better only 55 percent of the time. On the other occasions, the market price collapsed even further than the NAV did. The evidence shows that, on most occasions, a discount can't be counted upon to provide protection against steep NAV losses. So don't let a large discount provide you with too much of a false sense of security about an investment, for there are many other factors to consider.

Selecting a good closed-end foreign fund is hard work. It's already enough of a challenge to identify funds that have good long-term records, able management, and appropriate strategies, and that are selling at decent prices. A fund's ability to offset the risks of currency fluctuations through hedging techniques is worth noting, yet determining whether a particular hedging strategy is valid is generally a tricky business. Most investors might be better off picking a good fund that hedges rarely or not at all. Some funds consistently made incorrect currency calls, and their returns have been significantly damaged as a result. The penalty for faulty tactics can throw a fund's results far behind those of an unhedged fund that simply rolled with the currency punches. Morningstar research has shown that currency exposure isn't nearly as important a consideration when selecting a foreign closed-end fund as fundamental traits, such as sector weightings and prospects for the fund's market of choice. In the case of emerging-market funds, there simply aren't many funds hedging their currency exposure to choose from to begin with.

CLASSIC CLOSED-END FUNDS WITH LONG-TERM TRACK RECORDS

MEXICO FUND
Seeks long-term capital appreciation by investing in securities listed on the Mexican Stock Exchange. Above-average return with high risk. Portfolio manager José Luis Gómez-Pimienta (since 1981). Shares traded on the New York Stock Exchange. Ticker symbol MXF. Ten-year annualized NAV total return through 1995 of 24.89 percent.

TEMPLETON EMERGING MARKETS
Seeks long-term capital appreciation by investing at least 75 percent of assets in emerging countries. Above-average return with average risk. Portfolio manager Mark Mobius (since 1987). Shares traded on the NYSE. Ticker symbol EMF. From fund inception in February 1987, annualized NAV total return of 19.43 percent.

ASIA PACIFIC
Seeks long-term capital appreciation by investing at least 80 percent of assets in Hong Kong, Korea, Malaysia, the Philippines, Singapore, Taiwan, and Thailand. Above-average return with average risk. Portfolio manager David Brennan (since 1987). Shares traded on the NYSE. Ticker symbol APB. From fund inception in May 1987, annualized NAV total return of 15.52 percent.

CENTRAL SECURITIES
Seeks capital appreciation by investing primarily in common stocks, but may invest in convertibles, preferreds, and debt securities. Buys companies with high earnings-growth rates at value prices. High return with below-average risk. Portfolio manager Wilmot Kidd (since 1973). Shares traded on American Stock Exchange. Ticker symbol CET. Ten-year annualized NAV total return of 17.17 percent.

TRI-CONTINENTAL
Seeks growth of capital and income while producing reasonable current income, primarily through dividend-paying domestic stocks. Average return with average risk. Portfolio manager Charles Smith (since 1995). Shares traded on NYSE. Ticker symbol TY. Ten-year annualized NAV total return of 13.73 percent.

SOURCE CAPITAL
Seeks capital appreciation for its common stockholders consistent with current income to meet the dividend on its preferred shares. Favors companies with large profit margins that use their profits either to expand through acquisitions or repurchase shares. Average return with low risk. Portfolio manager George Michaelis (since 1977). Shares traded on NYSE. Ticker symbol SOR. Ten-year annualized NAV total return of 11.13 percent.

ADAMS EXPRESS
Primary objective is preservation of capital through defensive stocks. Best for conservative investors willing to forgo some upside potential. Average return with below-average risk. Portfolio manager Douglas Ober (since 1986). Shares traded on NYSE. Ticker symbol ADX. Ten-year annualized NAV total return of 13.71 percent.

SWISS HELVETIA
Seeks long-term capital appreciation by investing primarily in equity and debt securities of Swiss companies. Above-average return with above-average risk. Portfolio manager Georges de Montebello (since 1987). Shares traded on NYSE. Ticker symbol SWZ. Annualized NAV return of 9.16 percent since inception in August 1987.

KOREA FUND
Seeks capital appreciation by investing at least 80 percent of assets in securities listed on the Korean Stock Exchange. Above-average return with average risk. Portfolio manager John Lee (since 1991). Traded on NYSE. Ticker symbol KF. Ten-year annualized NAV return of 24.03 percent.

NUVEEN MUNICIPAL VALUE
Seeks current income exempt from regular federal income tax by investing 80 percent of assets in tax-exempt municipal obligations rated BBB or better. Below-average return with below-average risk. Portfolio manager Thomas Spalding (since 1987). Traded on NYSE. Ticker symbol NUV. Annualized NAV total return of 8.55 percent since inception in August 1987.

NEWER CLOSED-END FUNDS
WORTH WATCHING

NEW AGE MEDIA. Portfolio manager John Gillespie. Traded on NYSE. Ticker symbol NAF. Up 44.65 percent in NAV total return in 1995.

FIRST FINANCIAL. Portfolio manager Nicholas Adams. Traded on NYSE. Ticker symbol FF. Five-year annualized NAV return of 52.46 percent through 1995.

SOUTHEASTERN THRIFT & BANK. Portfolio manager James Schmidt. Traded over-the-counter. Ticker symbol STBF. Five-year annualized NAV return of 40.34 percent.

H&Q HEALTHCARE INVESTORS. Portfolio manager Alan Carr. Traded on NYSE. Ticker symbol HQH. Five-year annualized NAV return of 19.23 percent.

COHEN & STEERS TOTAL RETURN. Portfolio managers Martin Cohen and Robert Steers. Traded on NYSE. Ticker symbol RFI. Up 9.20 percent in NAV total return in 1995.

HIGH YIELD PLUS. Portfolio manager Catherine Smith. Traded on NYSE. Ticker symbol HYP. Five-year annualized NAV return of 19.63 percent.

BEA STRATEGIC INCOME. Portfolio manager Richard Lindquist. Traded on NYSE. Ticker symbol FBI. Five-year annualized NAV return of 14.19 percent.

MORGAN STANLEY ASIA-PACIFIC. Portfolio manager Ean Wah Chin. Traded on NYSE. Ticker symbol APF. Up 9.18 percent in NAV total return in 1995.

SOUTHERN AFRICA FUND. Portfolio manager Mark Breedon. Traded on NYSE. Ticker symbol SOA. Up 31.49 percent in NAV total return in 1995.

CZECH REPUBLIC FUND. Portfolio managers Pierre Daviron and Elisa Mazen. Traded on NYSE. Ticker symbol CRF. Decline in NAV of 1.68 percent in 1995.

TAKING STOCK

Stocks are hardly a difficult-to-find investment. News reports blare out the latest records set on major exchanges, whether bull market triumphs or bear market tumbles. Brokers beckon in advertisements and through telephone calls. Though all of this might seem overwhelming, investors who have entered the market through stock mutual funds would be wise to study the individual stocks held in their funds more closely to see which ones might fit their needs, and to consider adding some of them to their personal portfolio. If you can study mutual funds, you can analyze a company and its stock. They're interconnected. The goal is to study as much as you can so you can compare a variety of stocks to each other and choose those right for your goals, just as you would with any other investment. You can do it yourself once you grow beyond the hot tips and overhyped sales pitches. The *Morningstar International Stocks* binder product covering 720 stocks and *On Demand* fax/mail product developed by Morningstar have become leaders in coverage of overseas equities by offering performance figures, commentaries, analysis, and other pertinent information. For example, to show the ties between stocks and funds, each company report in *International Stocks* lists the seven mutual funds with the largest positions in it. The introduction of U.S. Equities OnFloppy software covering 7,500 stocks is Morningstar's first step in coverage of individual U.S. stocks, the result of purchasing another company for its database. It is purely a data product without commentary.

Times and attitudes are changing in the stock world. Americans currently own more than $350 billion in foreign stock, with about 70 percent of that amount accumulated during the 1990s as they became more aware of the many investment opportunities beyond our shores, according to the Securities Industry Association. Investors are becoming more sophisticated and less parochial in their views about business and markets worldwide.

"Ultimately an investor ends up buying a stock not because it comes from a certain country, but because it is a better buy, has a better growth rate, or some other advantage over its counterparts in the same industry," said Catherine Gillis Odelbo, publisher of *Morningstar Equities*. "The bottom line is that all of these companies are competing against each other."

International stocks provide opportunities, especially those that are sold on U.S. exchanges as American Depositary Receipts (ADRs). These are for investors who still like the idea of selecting a specific company in which to put their money. ADRs are negotiable certificates that represent ownership of a given number of shares in a foreign company. They were created in the 1920s to satisfy investor demand for a simple way to invest in foreign securities. In the past decade, the market has grown rapidly and become one of the most popular vehicles by which U.S. investors hold shares in foreign corporations. There are now about 1,000 ADRs on the market, representing underlying shares trading in more than fifty countries. *Morningstar International Stocks* covers about 600 of the most actively traded ADRs, ranging from blue-chip companies in the

United Kingdom and Japan to explosive firms in emerging markets such as Mexico and Brazil. In addition, it covers about 120 foreign companies, many of them Canadian, that are listed directly on U.S. exchanges.

Issued by depositary banks in the United States, ADRs trade on U.S. exchanges or on the over-the-counter market and behave exactly like other U.S. securities. When investors place an order through a broker, they receive a certificate signifying that shares of that foreign company are being held by a custodian bank in the company's home market. An ADR can represent one share, be a fraction of an underlying share, or be the equivalent of several shares. They're denominated in U.S. dollars and the depositary bank makes all dividend payments to investors in dollars. The bank handles most of the paperwork and supplies ADR holders with disclosure materials, such as annual reports. Besides the fees charged by the depositary bank, investors usually must pay foreign taxes on dividend income, though they may file to receive an offsetting credit on their U.S. returns. The three largest depositary banks are Morgan Guaranty, Bank of New York, and Citibank.

ADR programs can be either sponsored or unsponsored. The sponsored programs, which account for the majority of newly created ADRs, are initiated by the company that issues the underlying shares. Unsponsored programs are initiated by a depositary bank and represent a majority of all ADRs, although few are being created today. In sponsored programs, the company pays many of the administrative expenses and is more directly involved in seeing that investors receive disclosure documents and other important information. A company may decide to have its ADRs listed on a U.S. exchange such as the New York Stock Exchange, American Stock Exchange, or NASDAQ. Most ADRs that aren't listed trade on the OTC Bulletin Board as "pink sheet" listings.

Companies with ADRs generally report their complete financial statements according to the accounting conventions in their home market. Very few convert their books to U.S. Generally Accepted Accounting Principles (GAAP) for ADR investors, although partial U.S. GAAP figures are usually available for companies with ADRs on major U.S. exchanges. The U.S. Securities and Exchange Commission requires these companies to file 20-F annual reports, which are similar to the 10-Ks filed by U.S. companies.

Tax is always a consideration in any investment. A recurrent item for holders of foreign equities is the withholding tax levied by foreign governments. For most countries it's a straight 15 percent. However, there's no withholding tax in Argentina, Hong Kong, and Mexico, while in Chile it can be as much as 30 percent. The good news is that U.S. investors eventually get this money back from the U.S. government, since the U.S. has agreements with most countries not to double-tax dividends. Basically, that situation is that if the foreign government taxes them, then the U.S. won't. To reclaim the portion of their dividends withheld by foreign governments, U.S. investors must file IRS Form 1116 along with their federal income tax returns.

Foreign currency exposure definitely has its ups and downs. Mexico's currency plummeted in the early and mid-1980s because of the country's debt crisis; the mark and the yen skyrocketed in the mid-1980s following the Group of Seven's decision to talk down the U.S. dollar; European currencies, including the pound, lira, and peseta, got clobbered in 1992 when Europe's monetary system broke down. As pointed out earlier in this chapter, it's not a good idea to try to get too clever by jumping in and out of international investments to avoid weak currencies. "Foreign stocks, particularly those from emerging markets, can be expected to perform better than U.S. stocks over the next five, ten, or twenty years, but not over a few months," Haywood Kelly, editor of *Morningstar International Stocks*, wrote in a commentary. "There's no sense in trying to avoid this volatility—it goes with the territory. The best one can do is minimize the risks through broad diversification and a long-term perspective, and grit one's teeth during the periodic rough spots."

To correct for the distortions that exchange rate fluctuations can cause, Morningstar calculates growth rates in local currency, which appear on each company report page. Another persistent concern in a number of countries is the effect of inflation. To resist the spell cast by "voodoo" growth, Morningstar also provides each country's historical movement of exchange rates and its historical record of inflation. It recommends that, when considering an international stock, you determine how long growth has continued by comparing three-year, five-year, and ten-year growth rates. Other considerations such as debt, accounting, earnings per ADR, and dividends are also important, Morningstar has found.

At some point, Morningstar expects it will change the focus of its international stock publications to place stocks in various business categories, rather than arrange them as it currently does by countries. Regional barriers are gradually melting away as individual investors focus on what's really important: profits, dividends, and stock appreciation. Those concepts are certainly understandable in any language.

Whether mutual funds, variable annuities, closed-end funds, or individual stocks, there will always be accompanying myths with no ties to reality. Once those myths have been exploded, the investor can get on with constructing a diverse personal portfolio that can prosper in any economic or market environment.

INTERNATIONAL STOCKS (ADRS) WITH THE BEST TRACK RECORD

HUTCHISON WHAMPOA

Hong Kong–based international conglomerate in telecommunications, property investment, energy, retail, and finance businesses. Large-capitalization growth stock with average risk. Sold over-the-counter. U.S. ticker symbol HUWHY. Five-year average return through 1995 of 32.33 percent; earnings-per-share growth of 17.30 percent.

BARRICK GOLD

Canadian-based gold-mining company is the largest outside South Africa. Large-cap growth stock with above-average risk. Sold on NYSE. U.S. ticker symbol ABX. Five-year average return of 26.55 percent; EPS growth 46.50 percent.

L'ORÉAL

World's largest producer of cosmetic products, perfumes, and hair care products. Based in France. Large-cap growth stock with average risk. Sold over-the-counter. U.S. ticker symbol LORLY. Five-year average return of 24.89 percent; EPS growth 10.20 percent.

HONG KONG TELECOMMUNICATIONS

Runs communication and information technology businesses in Hong Kong. Large-cap growth stock with average risk. Sold on NYSE. U.S. ticker symbol HKT. Five-year average return of 24.34 percent; EPS growth 14.80 percent.

HEINEKEN

Produces and distributes beer, wine, spirits, and soft drinks in more than 170 countries. Based in the Netherlands. Large-cap growth and value stock with below-average risk. Sold on NYSE. U.S. ticker symbol HINKY. Five-year average return of 23.36 percent; EPS growth 13.10 percent.

REUTERS

British company provides financial data, news, historical databases, and information management systems to business and the news media. Large-cap growth stock with below-average risk. Sold on NASDAQ. U.S. ticker symbol RTSY. Five-year average return of 21.93 percent; EPS growth 14.80 percent.

EMPRESA NACIONAL DE ELECTRICIDAD

Electric utility that serves more than 3 million customers and accounts for 27 percent of Spain's electricity output. Large-cap value stock with average risk. Sold on NYSE. U.S. ticker symbol ELE. Five-year average return of 18.72 percent; EPS growth 13.10 percent.

NOVO NORDISK

Danish manufacturer of pharmaceuticals and bioindustrial products. Medium-cap growth and value stock with below-average risk. Sold on NYSE. U.S. ticker symbol NVO. Five-year average return of 14.98 percent; EPS growth 10.10 percent.

NESTLÉ

Swiss firm is one of the world's largest food producers and a leading producer of beverages, dairy products, pharmaceuticals, and pet foods. Large-cap growth and value stock with below-average risk. Sold over-the-counter. U.S. ticker symbol NSRGY. Five-year average return of 13.94 percent; EPS growth 5 percent.

BOOTS

British developer, producer, and marketer of health and personal care products. Large-cap value stock with average risk. Sold over-the-counter. U.S. ticker symbol BOOOY. Five-year average return of 10.59 percent; EPS growth 20.80 percent.

CHAPTER 12

■

THE TAX MAN

"One senior officer of a large fund company once told me, 'I wouldn't want to shackle my traders with having to worry about taxes.' What he, in effect, was saying was, 'I don't think the wallets of my shareholders really matter.'"
—PATRICK GEDDES, MORNINGSTAR
CHIEF FINANCIAL OFFICER

The buck often starts and stops right here.

"Y-e-s!" shouted a product support team leader wearing a gray T-shirt and sweat-shorts. He raised a triumphant fist and then executed a pirouette on the way back to his desk. His telephone-operator-style headset with protruding mouthpiece remained clamped firmly to his head during that ballet-like feat. Another question had been answered to a caller's satisfaction and a subscription had been logged. As the leader exulted, fellow workers talked nonstop to other subscribers and would-be subscribers on telephones in their respective cubicles.

More than 1,200 phone calls are handled each day by the thirty-one product support staffers and eight technical support workers assigned by Morningstar to take new orders, field inquiries about subscriptions, arrange delivery, and answer both technical and investment questions regarding products.

"We don't want this operation to be a sweatshop and we don't want anyone to just be 'Julie the operator' taking orders like in the magazine subscription commercials on TV, " said Kelly Rhoten-Miszuk, head of the product support area, as she walked down an aisle of cubicles amid a cacophony of ringing telephones. "We hire college graduates with financial interests because, since we initiated a full product support staff in 1989, we find that callers are becoming more educated and much more aware of mutual funds."

What questions about funds do subscribers and potential subscribers ask when their curiosity extends beyond subscriptions or computer disks?

Increasingly, there are questions about taxes, an issue that is only now coming to the forefront in mutual fund investing. While total returns still grab the headlines, more and more mutual fund investors sense they're paying more in taxes on their funds than they really should.

If taxes happen to pique your interest, this chapter is for you. Read on. If not, well, you had your chance. Proceed directly to Chapter 13.

Taxation is a vital consideration when selecting investments, even though most mutual fund companies would rather you simply forget all about it. Remember that in basic tax planning the after-tax return is the profit you actually get to keep, and that your tax liability depends on your entire tax situation, especially your personal tax bracket. A fund is more tax-efficient if it has a high percentage of total profit from appreciation of its net asset value (NAV), a low percentage of total profit from capital gains distribution, and the lowest percentage of total profit from ordinary income. Too often, an investor focuses on a fee of 1 percent or less when choosing among funds, while completely overlooking that he may wind up paying Uncle Sam an amount that's five to ten times that amount. The difference that taxes make in fund returns becomes particularly evident in a period in which overall returns are less than impressive.

While it's unwise to ignore tax analysis, it's still not the first item an investor should have in mind when selecting a fund. Don't put the cart before the horse. Tax analysis should come only after an investor has made major decisions in regard to asset class, manager selection, sector exposure, and risk profile. You still want to find a fund with a good return, but you want to be sure you'll be able to keep as much of that return as possible. Fund companies have been hostile to the idea of emphasizing tax considerations because, in their eyes, it's a negative concept that complicates the investment. In fact, Morningstar has discovered that a number of funds don't even bother in their internal accounting to do individual share identification for their own capital gains. As a result, they're paying out more capital gains than they need to be paying out. It seems they don't care enough about their shareholders to consider taxes.

There is, thankfully, a growing awareness of the role of taxes associated with funds, thanks in part to media coverage, academic research, and the efforts of Morningstar. Companies such as Vanguard Group and Charles Schwab are now actually selling index funds specifically designed to excel in tax-adjusted performance, this generally accomplished through procedures such as holding appreciated securities to avoid capital gains distributions and selling off losing stocks at the end of each month. Some competitors have actually taken them to task for "turning taxes into a marketing game" with these products. Others say that such rejiggering for tax concerns means these index products will less accurately reflect the stock indexes they seek to replicate. Yet the concept behind what these companies are doing is really something that the rest of the industry should be working on as well. A tax-advantaged fund concept is only a fad if taxes themselves become a fad. Given our federal government's ongoing penchant for taxation, that seems highly unlikely.

TAXATION BASICS

Fully understand the tax implications of your mutual funds. There are two levels of taxation. First, the fund receives income and generates capital gains on its trades. Secondly, there's the investor's taxability. This includes ordinary income in the form of dividends from the fund, as well as capital gains from either a distribution from the fund or an investor's sale of shares. For most mutual fund investors, this relationship between tax and a fund is a vague concept that's hardly ever a consideration when purchasing shares in a fund.

"The investor should look at the mutual fund as a conduit which passes all the tax effects through to the investor," explained Patrick Geddes, Morningstar's chief financial officer and former director of quantitative analysis. "While you're getting the advantages of diversification, liquidity, and professional management with a mutual fund, there's also a disadvantage versus holding individual securities in that you're giving up control of the tax timing." If financial analysts for U.S. corporations ran their cash flow analysis on a pretax basis, they'd lose their jobs, Geddes contends. While corporations consider taxes in every analysis, that philosophy just hasn't trickled down to the retail investor. This point is obvious to Geddes, a thirty-eight-year-old University of Chicago M.B.A., because he was previously employed as a financial analyst in the treasurer's department of a major oil company both in Chicago and Switzerland. Corporate finance taught him that a tax expense is a dollar outflow just like any other.

TYPE OF ACCOUNT

Of course, where you hold the investment matters most in terms of tax consequences. The biggest tax consideration of all is whether your mutual fund is in an individual retirement account, 401(k) retirement account, variable annuity, or taxable account. High tax bracket investors are obviously going to want to hold their highest income-producing assets in tax-exempt accounts. In doing an analysis of whether you should hold, you must look at your entire portfolio. You want your lower tax liabilities in taxable accounts, and the higher tax liability in tax-exempt accounts. If you have a stock fund with a high return, you don't necessarily know if you want to have that in your taxable or tax-exempt account because it depends on how much tax liability the fund is generating. Let's say you have a stock fund that's earning 10 percent and a bond fund earning 8 percent. If the stock fund is paying everything out and you're in a 28 percent tax bracket, you'd rather have the stock fund in your tax-exempt account. The bond fund, because of the tax difference between the very highest tax bracket and 28 percent, could be better placed in a tax-exempt account. Unfortunately, there's no one easy answer because everything ultimately depends on the individual's portfolio and tax situation. But never put a fund that's specifically designed to defer taxes into a tax-deferred account, because it will have a low income stream that would be best put in a taxable account.

It should be noted that investors can refer to the tax analysis section of each *MMF* page to examine individual funds' after-tax returns and tax efficiency, which shows how much of the fund's returns investors keep after paying taxes on the distributions. The overview pages at the beginning of each stock group objective permit a comparison that makes it easy to see if a fund ranks above or below average on an after-tax basis. Drawing in the potential capital gain exposure statistic can help give investors an even better idea about how much appreciation the fund is sitting on. It can help determine if a manager change or rush of redemptions leads a fund to realize significant gains.

TAXING CONSIDERATIONS

In taxable accounts, everything else being equal, the long-term investor should minimize fund payouts in order to control tax timing. By focusing on the NAV, determine what portion of a fund's total taxable return is controlled by the shareholder and what portion is controlled by the fund. For a tax advantage, most likely you'll be looking at stock funds rather than fixed-income funds and especially those with low dividend payments, low turnover, and a high rate of appreciation in NAV. The worst type of fund from a tax standpoint is one that generates a lot of dividends or interest payments because there's no way to defer income and the income will be taxed at the investor's tax bracket. A straight taxable bond fund or any kind of income fund falls into this group. Another tax-inefficient fund is one in which the capital gains are distributed on an ongoing basis. Because it's trading so much, it has to pay out nearly everything it makes in capital gains in order to avoid a special excise tax. This type of fund distributes most of its capital appreciation annually.

Basic tax analysis is, after all, built around timing. As in any financial planning, you want cash inflows as soon as possible and cash outflows as late as possible. You want to defer tax liability because of the time value. In the long run, even after liquidating an account after many years, you're always going to end up paying some amount of tax, except in cases in which the investment goes directly into an estate. For tax efficiency, a fund's payout should be low and its NAV appreciation high.

For example, consider two equity funds, Fidelity Value Fund and the William Blair Growth Fund, and the implications primarily for a long-term investor likely to hold the funds for more than ten years. Looking at pretax returns on a ten-year annualized return basis, William Blair Growth produced a 12.5 percent annual return, while Fidelity Value was 12.2 percent. But on an after-tax basis, Fidelity Value came out on top with a 9.2 percent after-tax annualized return, compared to 8.9 percent for William Blair Growth. The major difference between the two funds, then, is the NAV appreciation over the last ten years. The Fidelity fund's NAV has more than doubled, while the William Blair fund's NAV slightly declined. (This example factors in a 31 percent tax rate on ordinary income and 28 percent on capital gains.)

Here's a hypothetical example that shows the long-term effects of taxes. Let's say you invest $10,000 in two different mutual funds and both have an annual total return (all capital gains) of 10 percent. The first fund, with an annual distribution of 10 percent, will have a balance after twenty years of $40,169. Its net asset value would rise during the course of each year and the distribution would have brought it back down, providing a flat NAV in the process. You have no control over the tax timing in that case. Meanwhile, the second fund, with no annual distribution, will wind up with a greater balance of $51,238. The deferred account over time handily beat the one paying out regularly. Both examples given include tax payments upon closing of the account and assume a 28 percent tax rate on capital gains. Implications would be even greater for someone in a higher tax bracket. It's worth noting that the final numbers most of all will be dependent on an individual investor's tax bracket.

DISTRIBUTION DILEMMA

You can have some control if you take an active tax management stance, although it will require more effort in bookkeeping, planning, and figuring out the tax implications. As you move a bit deeper into the tax issue, realize that the concept of potential capital gains exposure is sometimes misused when some experts say a long-term investor shouldn't buy into a fund that may be making a huge distribution because he may be accelerating some of his tax payments. Take as an extreme case a fund with 40 percent of its value in unrealized gains. If it has a new manager and liquidates the portfolio to accommodate his new style, it makes a large distribution. The investor must pay tax on that as soon as the fund makes the distribution. What's left out in that particular analysis, however, is the fact that tax-efficient funds may show a big buildup. If you never have any potential capital gain exposure in a fund, that's because you've either been paying out all your distributions, have been losing money, or have a flood of new money coming in.

Another crucial consideration is that, if you buy into a fund that subsequently makes a large distribution, you have some control over it because of your tax basis. If you buy it at $10 a share on December 15 and the next day the fund makes a $4 distribution, your NAV essentially drops to $6 as a result. Assuming there is no change in the actual value, you're going to pay tax on this for that tax year. However, if you sold on December 16 at $6, your tax basis is $10 and your sales price will be $6. That means you have a loss of $4 and a gain of $4 and you just offset the effect. That dramatizes the fact that if you do get into a fund which makes a distribution that is larger than your actual gain, you can reverse the effect.

It's generally better to buy in after a distribution has been made by the fund. If a fund has only a 5 to 10 percent capital gain exposure, you needn't worry about it and it shouldn't necessarily keep you out of that fund. You can generally find out, particularly late in the year, the amount that a fund is going to distribute and can avoid buying in until immediately afterward. Don't be totally scared away by a large capital gain exposure. Pay attention to it, but never think that a large potential capital gains exposure is totally bad.

BEING EFFICIENT

Unfortunately, tax efficiency sometimes isn't all that predictable, Morningstar research has found. It's only sure to be reliable if there is a strong reason to believe a fund will be tax-efficient, as in the case of an index fund or a tax-managed account with low payout. As far as asset classes are concerned, the more income you have, the less tax-efficient you will be. Riskier small-company, aggressive growth, and foreign funds tend to be the most tax-efficient because they emphasize price appreciation rather than an income stream. As you move down the continuum toward conservatism, there is less tax efficiency, especially in taxable bonds. Taxable high-yield junk bonds are among the most tax-inefficient of all funds because they have considerable capital fluctuation but always give a regular payout. You may be earning 15 percent or losing 10 percent, but you're always paying an ordinary income tax bill every year and may have some capital gains on top of that. For that reason, junk bonds are excellent investment candidates for tax-sheltered individual retirement accounts. When considering municipal bond funds, look closely at how much of the total return comes from tax-exempt income and how much comes from taxable capital gain. That's especially critical in a falling interest rate environment when many of the bonds are now worth more than they were when initially purchased.

CAPITAL GAINS

The efficient way of managing existing capital gains is to track all purchases of shares and specify the exact shares you wish to sell to minimize the tax impact. Select the highest basis, which gives you the smallest gain, and defer the payments on larger capital gains. Deferral may not add up to significant savings in the short run, but the longer-term tax difference can be substantial.

In the calculation of capital gains, there's a complicated way and an easier way. The more complicated way is the one in which you can save the most money. In the individual share identification when you're selling only part of your holdings in a fund, you want to identify the highest cost-basis shares and sell them first in order to minimize your tax. Some people keep it simple by keeping each mutual fund account a small enough size so that they can liquidate them in their entirety and not have to deal with this. Another way to do the calculation of capital gains is on an average basis where you simply throw together everything you bought over time, including distributions. Just take an average across that period. Some fund companies will do this calculation for you, which is a real plus.

Some people may not realize that, if they've been paying taxes over a long period of time, their basis upon sale is the original investment amount plus all of the distributions upon which they've been paying taxes. Be sure that when you're selling the fund and you calculate the capital gains, you have the proceeds amount and also your basis. For something more simple like a stock, your basis is just what you paid for it. For a mutual fund, it is what you paid for it, plus all the reinvested distributions you have received over the time you held the fund. Think of a reinvested dividend as though the fund sent you a check and you used it to buy more shares. You're adding up the total of the investment whether original or reinvestments. You already paid taxes on those reinvestments. If you don't count those in your basis, then you're paying taxes again—in fact, double-paying on the same income. It is not really the law that is complicated, but rather the structuring and distribution pattern.

Bear in mind that a reinvested distribution is not like a dividend from a stock. When you consider all the assets of a fund, think of the distribution as just one little piece carved out and given to you separately. Your wealth is still the sum of the two pieces. That's what the issue of funds and taxes is all about.

GETTING ACTIVE

There are other ways to actively manage your tax liabilities in funds. For example, there are "tax swaps," a way to cash in on unrealized losses. Investors with bond portfolio losses often swap for other higher-yielding bonds to be able to increase the return on their portfolio and realize tax losses by selling a fund with an unrealized loss and buying a similar fund as a temporary replacement. Beware of the "wash sale" rule regarding the purchase and sale of a security either simultaneously or within a short period of time. Wash sales taking place within thirty days of the underlying purchase don't qualify as tax losses under Internal

Revenue Service rules. The "Most Similar Funds" statistic on the *MMF* page helps you to find a fund that replicates the fund that you didn't want to hold through the end of the year. You want to make sure that if you're doing a swap it is worth the hassle. For example, if you're only going to save $14 in taxes, it's probably not worth the tax filing.

You can obtain from mutual fund companies the dates on which they pay their distributions. For most equity funds both ordinary and capital gains are in December. Income funds often pay quarterly or monthly. The overriding consideration is that mutual fund investments should be tied into an individual's overall tax plan. They're only a component of the total effect of taxation on their investment income.

Estate taxes are an important consideration, especially for wealthy individuals with significant estates. The basic "step up" rule for estate taxation essentially says that if you buy an asset at $10 a share, hold it for a number of years, and it is worth $120 a share when you die, your heirs can sell it at a tax basis of $120 a share. The government loses the taxation on that gain, even when it is realized, because the tax basis gets stepped up from $10 to $120. Another wrinkle involves 401(k) and IRAs in that when they are taxed, they're taxed completely as ordinary income. If you're in a high tax bracket and in an IRA where you're going to be pulling money out of soon, be sure that you're not converting capital gain income into ordinary income, which would have a negative effect. Once again, that's only a consideration that high-bracket individuals need to work on.

Another finer point of tax planning is the fact that bond funds have a choice of whether or not to amortize premiums. Most choose not to do so because it makes their yield look better, even though it's less tax-efficient. Converting current ordinary loss into deferred capital loss is bad because loss ideally should actually be accelerated. Furthermore, shifting loss from ordinary income to capital gains creates inefficiency because you want your losses to be in the highest tax category. The size and volume of the bond premiums bond funds are paying can be easily noted if you see an eroding NAV. This can be a sign that the fund is issuing high-coupon payouts that don't reflect current interest rates. Any portfolio manager that simply says that yield sells is overlooking the tax-inefficiency of that statement.

Factoring in tax considerations does complicate the mutual fund research process, but it's smart to spend the extra time after you've already gone down a checklist of other important fund considerations. You can't avoid taxes, but you may as well do a little extra homework so you can minimize their impact on your mutual funds and be fully prepared when they do bite.

CHAPTER 13

■

INVESTING WITH
AN ATTITUDE

"I have made this letter longer than usual because I lack the time to make it short."
—Philosopher and mathematician Blaise
Pascal in *The Provincial Letters,* written in 1656,
a sentiment that Morningstar president
Don Phillips considers instructive about
today's flood of investment information

When Morningstar was started in the living room of a one-bedroom apartment in 1984, society's burning question was: How can I get good information?

Today's question takes on a more urgent tone: How do I deal with my information overload?

Investing, like every other field in our computerized, multimedia world, is drowning in data and advice. It's as though the basic relationship between an individual and

239

money has been so dramatically altered by new instruments, financial markets, and modern communication that it's become too complex to grasp.

Don't buy into that philosophy. Investing can be done more easily and efficiently than ever before and the myriad of choices actually offers more flexibility. Mutual funds can make your task easier, not more difficult. Your strategy must include the same financial common sense that has always made good sense. That's part of the Morningstar approach to investing.

Call it investing with "an attitude." Morningstar's irreverent, youthful perspective on mutual funds discourages taking anything at face value. If someone tells you exactly what you want to hear, do your homework to find out whether it's true. If you don't watch out, the hype will kill you. Wiring into the mutual fund revolution is serious business.

Here are the no-nonsense Morningstar principles of mutual fund investing for investors of all ages:

1. Every investor must be a skeptic. Advertisements will never tell you what could go wrong with a mutual fund. It's up to you to find out how it has performed in difficult times.

2. You must trust in your own common sense. The investment world can be extremely arrogant. Just as a doctor wouldn't mock you for not knowing what a clavicle is, someone in finance shouldn't belittle you if you can't give a perfect definition of a Ginnie Mae.

3. Jargon is a warning signal. The more incomprehensible the investment-ese used by a portfolio manager, the less that manager really knows and the less defined the fund's goals will probably be.

4. No one should ever be panicked into an investment decision. It isn't important whether you make the decision now or a month from now, so long as you do invest at some point and continue to do so on a regular basis.

5. Mutual funds cannot be considered static investments. They must be monitored periodically so that what you *think* you own is actually what you own. Portfolio managers come and go, and philosophies evolve.

6. Not every investor needs a financial planner, but more investors need one than think they do. It's not a sign of weakness to ask for help if you need it.

7. The most important investment questions you can ask are about yourself, not the investment. You have the ability to answer when the college tuition check is due and when you want to retire. Handle those first, rather than broad macroeconomic questions such as where the Dow Jones industrial average will finish next year.

8. A series of good mutual funds may not build a good portfolio. Those funds might not fit your individual investment goals or provide proper diversification, even though each ranks highly against its peers.

9. Buying funds off the latest short-term top funds list is dangerous. Funds often get to the top of such lists by taking more risks than their competitors. In addition, funds appearing on leader lists at the same time likely took similar risks, so that a portfolio comprised of them may simply include different shadings of the same style.

10. The easiest way for a fund to be number one in its category is for it to be miscategorized. Make sure a fund's name and category are in keeping with the way it is actually managed. Many are not, so you should be on guard.

11. Before buying a fund, you must determine whether the people and practices that built the fund's record are still in place. Even a factor such as significant growth in a fund's assets may alter its management style.

12. There's no one right way to manage money. Different approaches work for different managers. Look for the right match between a portfolio and a manager, making sure the manager is willing to stick with that approach even when it's unpopular.

13. All investment approaches will fall in and out of favor. Don't chase after the hot styles after they've been bid up in price. Look for good managers in out-of-favor disciplines.

14. Investing is a means to an end, not an end in and of itself. If your investments help you meet your family's financial goals, you're a winner even if your return winds up to be less than the Standard & Poor's 500. This isn't a contest. It's about getting the most out of life.

INDEX

■

243

INDEX

INDEX

245

INDEX

INDEX

INDEX